GOD'S PURSUING LOVE

The Relentless Tenderness of God

JOHN WHITE

InterVarsity Press
Downers Grove, Illinois

InterVarsity Press
P.O. Box 1400, Downers Grove, IL 60515
World Wide Web: www.ivpress.com
E-mail: mail@ivpress.com

InterVarsity Press® is the book-publishing division of InterVarsity Christian Fellowship/USA®, a student movement active on campus at hundreds of universities, colleges and schools of nursing in the United States of America, and a member movement of the International Fellowship of Evangelical Students. For information about local and regional activities, write Public Relations Dept., InterVarsity Christian Fellowship/USA, 6400 Schroeder Rd., P.O. Box 7895, Madison, WI 53707-7895.

Cover photograph: SuperStock

ISBN 0-8308-1944-4

Printed in the United States of America ♾

Library of Congress Cataloging-in-Publication Data

White, John, 1924 Mar. 5-
    God's pursuing love : the relentless tenderness of God / John White.
        p.   cm.
    Includes bibliographical references.
    ISBN 0-8308-1944-4 (pbk. : alk. paper)
    1. God—Love—Biblical teaching. 2. Bible. O.T. Ruth—Theology.
3. Bible. N.T. Luke XV—Theology.   I. Title.
BS544.W45   1998
231'.6—dc21
                                                                    98-17437
                                                                        CIP

18	17	16	15	14	13	12	11	10	9	8	7	6	5	4	3	2
13	12	11	10	09	08	07	06	05	04	03	02	01	00	99	98	

To Ruth O'Hara

Prologue

We sometimes say, "The New is in the Old concealed, the Old is in the New revealed." We mean by this that the message of the New Testament is hidden in the Old Testament. We also mean that the message of the Old Testament is fully unveiled in the New Testament. The gospel of a loving God, his grace, his mercy, his kindness exists throughout the Bible, though it is made more explicit following the death, resurrection and ascension of Jesus. The same saving faith that Abraham displayed (Genesis 15:6), the same trust that Job revealed in a Redeemer God (Job 19:25), exists throughout the Bible even though its expression is fully realized only in Jesus.

The story of Ruth also plainly illustrates the gospel. In this important Old Testament book Naomi and Ruth are saved by a kinsman-redeemer. Ruth becomes pregnant *and bears a child.* Naomi loses her bitterness and becomes sanctified. She, Boaz and Ruth are among what used to be called "Old Testament saints."

Throughout Scripture the message is one of trust on our part and mercy, grace and kindness on God's part. Even our ability to trust is God-given and forms the channel by which his grace is mediated to us.

In the first four chapters of this book I expound the book of Ruth, chapter by chapter, illustrating the gospel/missionary application in each. Then in chapter five I illustrate the same gospel principles found in the first two of three parables found in Luke 15. I call the first parable The Seeking Shepherd. The second I call The Anxious Woman. These parables show how Jesus plainly taught salvation and sanctification.

In chapter six I consider the third parable in Luke 15. Usually referred to as The Prodigal Son, it could equally well be called The Waiting Father. The three parables illustrate the interaction of God and human beings. God seeks us with longing and love, but we must respond to his love. How it all works together—God's side and our own—is a mystery.

To God, who has purposes for her, Naomi is like a lost sheep, or a lost coin or a lost son. God wants her back. And since God is the Waiting Father, the Searching Shepherd, the Desperate Woman, there is still great hope for her. The good shepherd must find his sheep, the woman must find the coin, and the prodigal must come home to the Father. The book of Ruth perfectly reflects the principles of salvation that Jesus taught in Luke 15, which are all based on the longing of God for his people.

I suppose I could have illustrated the heart of the gospel by quoting the apostolic expositions of the theme, but it seems to me that the stories are more graphic. Jesus chose them for that reason, and so that he could focus on God's love toward sinful human beings. His delight in their return hits us powerfully.

1

Downhill to Bitterness

Still with unhurrying chase,
And unperturbed pace,
Deliberate speed, majestic instancy,
Came on the following feet,
And a voice above their beat—
"Naught shelters thee, who will not shelter Me."[1]

God pursues us to give us himself. He pursues us to teach us that he is the most important thing in life.

When we pursue God, often it is because we want something. But he will not necessarily give us exactly what we want. That may be because what we want will do us harm.

God loves and God pursues, as the poem "The Hound of Heaven" quoted above illustrates. But there are two sides to the question of divine love—God's and our own. We are pursued, and yet we return to God. God certainly does pursue. He has purposes in our lives, but his purposes call us to respond.

The Story Begins
The Old Testament book of Ruth is a story of pursuit, of God

pursuing his people, and of their response to him. It is a touching and lovely story, but one that begins with a tragedy. Naomi and her husband Elimelech are Hebrews who have moved to the foreign territory of Moab, southeast of the Dead Sea, to avoid being trapped in an area of famine.

In the very first verses of chapter 1 we read that Naomi's husband dies. She is then left with her two sons, who marry Moabite women named Orpah and Ruth. Ten years later her two sons also die, and she is left alone with her daughters-in-law. Her grief is great because she has lost those who are most precious to her. Yet her situation is more desperate still because she is without the protection and support of a male head of the family. In the world of the ancient Middle East this could leave her destitute and cut off from society. She has no security and little hope for income.

Naomi reacts as many in her situation might. She looks at the facts and the future before her, and she feels that God is against her. To her daughters-in-law she says, "It is more bitter for me than for you, because the LORD's hand has gone out against me!" (Ruth 1:13).

But God is pursuing Naomi. Embittered as she is, she recognizes God as one who punishes sin but not as one who longs for her. She does not understand what God is trying to teach her. She does not realize until very much later in her life that the Hound of Heaven pursued her even though she had lost her whole family. Her husband and her two sons apparently meant everything to her, so that *only when they were taken away from her* was she ready to see that when we have God, we have everything. When we don't have God, we have nothing worth having.

Naomi hears that "the LORD had come to the aid of his people by providing food for them" (1:6). So she decides to return to her home in Bethlehem. Her two daughters-in-law opt to accompany her. They have grown to love her, and she is company for them.

At first Naomi goes along with their idea of accompanying her on the long journey back to Bethlehem, but as they proceed she must have had second thoughts. Perhaps she recalls the hazards of the journey, her own initial difficulty in learning a new language and the ways of a new culture. Maybe she begins to see the situation from the perspective of her daughters-in-law; they might find another husband in Moab more easily than in Judah. Soon Naomi's thoughts find expression.

> Then Naomi said to her two daughters-in-law, "Go back, each of you, to your mother's home. May the LORD show kindness to you, as you have shown to your dead and to me. May the LORD grant that each of you will find rest in the home of another husband." (1:8-9)

The custom in those days was that when a man's brother died he was obligated to marry his widowed sister-in-law. But Naomi reminds her daughters-in-law that she has no sons nor any husband who could give her sons.

> Return home, my daughters. Why would you come with me? Am I going to have any more sons, who could become your husbands? Return home, my daughters; I am too old to have another husband. Even if I thought there was still hope for me—even if I had a husband tonight and then gave birth to sons—would you wait until they grew up? Would you remain unmarried for them? No, my daughters. (1:11-13)

Naomi had no other sons who could marry her daughters-in-law, nor does she know what possibilities of marriage the two women will have in Israel. Probably not far along on their journey, spurred by the memory of danger that she had forgotten, danger that would have been smaller had a man accompanied them, Naomi realizes that her companions would be better off in Moab. Quietly and firmly, she tells them that they had better turn back.

Ruth and Orpah weep and protest, saying that they would still go with her. But Naomi will have none of it. She knows the reality she has passed through. She has become a bitter realist, and so she talks reality. At this decision point the difference between Orpah and Ruth becomes apparent.

Orpah, at least, recognizes the common sense of Naomi's words and decides to heed her advice, but not without more tears and hugs. I imagine that many of us would be tearful under similar circumstances, but their farewell was more poignant than many of our own because the women did not expect to ever see each other again. Orpah kisses Naomi and departs—grief-stricken, but realistic enough to see quite clearly what the options are and what she prefers. She realizes that her own future will be better served in Moab, among her own people.

Ruth, on the other hand, refuses to do anything but cling to Naomi (1:14). In one of the most moving speeches of love and devotion found in all of biblical literature she declares, "Where you go I will go, and where you stay I will stay. Your people will be my people and your God my God" (1:16). Whether or not she is interested in Yahweh, the Lord, Ruth certainly makes a strong statement that she will adopt the beliefs of the Israelites, and that nothing but death can separate her from Naomi.

"Call Me Mara"

Some time later, two women approach the city of Bethlehem on foot. Had you been there, you would have seen that the older of the two has a face hardened by the blank look of despair and bitterness. The face of the younger, in contrast, bears mingled fear, curiosity and hope. The two little realize what God holds in store for them. Blind to future history, the two wend their unhurried way to the open city gates.

Their journey has been hard and long. Travel for unprotected women was even more difficult then than it is now. The distance between Moab and Bethlehem was lengthy and difficult. Roads were not exactly what we now call to mind by the term. They were crude, earthen and rough, little more than paths. Even Roman roads lay in the distant future. The two women would have had to circumvent the Dead Sea and would be hardened both by the rugged journey and by the dangers they had passed through.

As they enter the city gates of Bethlehem, a ripple of excitement slowly begins to break (1:19). Idle curiosity about the identity of the two women gives way to cries of wonder, recognition and stunned surprise. People gather round the two, exclaiming to one another. Heads turn. Conversing couples stop for a moment to stare. In the small town of Bethlehem at that time, everyone knew who everyone was. New faces were a novelty that drew a growing crowd. Sensing something afoot, townspeople open doors and emerge from houses, hurrying toward those already gathered around the women.

"It's Naomi, with a Moabite woman!"

"Naomi? Back in Bethlehem?"

"Naomi? Who is she?"

"Yes, Naomi. You know, she left here years ago with Elimelech. She's back! And with a young Moabite woman!"

Excitement is unusual in the little town, and news, precious.

"Can this really be Naomi? Where is her husband?"

But the older of the two newcomers gives vent to a bitter cry. "Don't call me Naomi," she says. "Call me Mara—bitter!"

Names in those days had significant meanings, and simply by stating this new name, Naomi tells her old friends how her life has gone.

"Oh, Naomi. Don't say that! Welcome back! Why bitter?"

"Because the Almighty has made my life very bitter."

"Why, Naomi? Why?"

"Can't you see? I went away full, but the Lord has brought me back empty."

"Yes, but the Lord is good, Naomi! Surely you don't mean that he has abandoned you?"

"Why call me Naomi? The LORD has afflicted me; the Almighty has brought misfortune upon me" (1:20-21).

The Famine

Most of us live far from famine. We see it only in TV newscasts. But to be present in a famine, to live under famine conditions, is a terrible experience that we in the West have on the whole been spared. Famines are divine judgments. God also sends floods and earthquakes. His judgment has many forms, and it touches every nation on the face of the earth.

The apostle Paul talks about the principle behind God's judgments in Romans 1. He explains that every person—including you and me—has an instinctive awareness that creation implies a Creator God. We may blind ourselves to this fact, but we are still fully responsible when we choose to ignore this Creator God in favor of our own desires. Plainly put, anything we place above God and his laws is idolatry—sin. And sin requires judgment on his part.

The wrath of God is being revealed from heaven against all the godlessness and wickedness of men who suppress the truth by their wickedness, since what may be known about

God is plain to them, because God has made it plain to them. For since the creation of the world God's invisible qualities—his eternal power and divine nature—have been clearly seen, being understood from what has been made, so that men are without excuse. (Romans 1:18-20)

We have no excuse for idolatry. Paul tells us that this has been true since time began. Confession and repentance can bring relief, but indulgence in sin brings judgment—sometimes on individuals in the form of a personal loss and sometimes on societies in the form of famines or other harsh "natural" disasters.

We in the West have had times of relative hardship, times when people get hungry, but that does not constitute famine. In a famine people die of starvation, sometimes en masse. Many are children, especially those fed at their starving mothers' breasts. Babies, children and older people are the first to die. Young married people bury them. Would a good God send a famine? Yes, he would. There are things God fears more than our deaths. He hates his chosen to be slaves to sin.

In the West we do not live in a time of starvation, but already judgments are falling on us. Christians surely can see that murder is on the increase and that we have been beset by floods, by unusual weather, by tragic bouts with tornadoes and by major catastrophes. We can see that society around us is steadily deteriorating. Major catastrophes both national and international are all around. Judgment affects countries, rulers and individuals. For Christians it can be not judgment but *discipline*.

The Facts of Judgment
Naomi's bitterness is an integral part of her salvation/sanctification. She understands that the Almighty has afflicted her. But she

cannot understand that God loves her with all the compassion of his heart. God is the father waiting on the rooftop, anxiously hoping for her return, the shepherd who seeks her everywhere. He wants her salvation to bring all its fruits to her. He loves her passionately—as he loves you. And if you are anything like me, to be passionately loved is very, very scary.

Naomi cannot understand what is happening. She has no idea what God has planned for her. Salvation/sanctification is also an ongoing experience that leads to a future deliverance, as Romans 5:10 tells us: "For if, when we were God's enemies, we were reconciled to him through the death of his Son, how much more, having been reconciled, shall we be saved through his life!" In a coming day we shall be delivered even from sin's presence. All three uses of the term *saved*—past, present and future—are valid.

Naomi is finding out that she is not in control of events but that a God of love is. God is the parent. Good parents hate to punish their children. This is true of God the Father. He grieves over people he loves, and he loves us all. People may not recognize God's judgment when it occurs. Do the floods and catastrophes of the present seem like judgments to people around us? Through the pain of his judgments God is shouting, seeking to attract our attention. Even Christians may not realize judgment (and discipline) can be part of a process, a judgment or a discipline that can sanctify. What is judgment for some is discipline for others, while still others will be delivered from it.

Anger and bitterness arise when we are powerless to do anything about what is happening around us. *We are bitter when we are in the dark.* And Naomi has been in the dark. She thought she was in control but was not. Either God is, or else we are. If I believe I am reasonably in control of my life when actually I am not, then I am in serious trouble indeed. For God will let me find out by the long, hard road of experience that he is the one who is in charge. God is often slow to react when he has purposes in someone's life.

So what *was* happening to Naomi's family? I believe the family itself was under judgment. Why?

Fact #1. The book of Judges (which precedes the book of Ruth and which covers the same period of Israel's history) reveals an endless series of judgments on Israel. Usually judgment took the form of Israel's subjugation by foreigners. On this occasion, it took the form of a famine. Judgment in the time of the judges was for idolatry—in the form of worship of the ancient god Baal. From idolatry every other sin arises. It gives rise to the neglect of the poor, the "me first" attitude, sexual sin, witchcraft and murder. Sooner or later every sin will appear in an idolatrous society.

Baal worship had been introduced to Israel by Balaam. Men would have sex with temple prostitutes, thus "giving their seed to the god" so that the fertility god would cause all seed to multiply. They hoped for abundant crops, productive livestock and many children.

The curious thing was that Israel did not clue in when the famine started. Rather than understanding that it was a judgment from God, the Israelites assumed they must support the false gods all the more. These were the gods they actually trusted. From the sidelines of history we can see that they had been taught that God alone was to be worshiped and that he would freely give them crops. His worship was to be shared by no other god (or fallen angel). But in the blindness of their condition they could not see what is so clear to us.

Many people—even professing Christians—do not realize they

worship Baal. They just see a prostitute, or have a little affair with a neighbor once in a while, confessing it to God afterward. Nothing serious. It's wrong, but we all sin once in a while. But in God's sight it constitutes idolatry, and idolatry blinds us. The same blindness was and still is on all who worshiped their own sexuality. Sex is good and a gift from God. But it is not to be used in worship of dark powers, but to be used thankfully and in the sanctity of marriage as God intended.

Fact #2. In the face of the famine, the family's choice of a country was Moab. If you were to ask people in Moab why they worshiped Baal, they immediately would say, "Baal worship works!" Certainly it seemed to at the time. And that is the precise answer Israelites, stricken as they were by famine, would have told you if they had talked as we now do. Moabites would have given local examples to illustrate the power of their god Baal. They did not see that at that point they were still the recipients of God's goodness—of the real and true mercy. God would wait until their cup of iniquity was full enough to bring judgment.

It is significant that in order to escape the judgment of famine, Elimelech's family had chosen Moab, a country of unadulterated idolatry, to which to make their escape. If they believed their Moabite neighbors, they too might have been worshiping Mammon and the fertility gods.

Fact #3. Elimelech died. Both his sons, who had married pagan wives, also died. The two sons died childless—a serious business in a rural community. Childlessness was regarded as a tragedy deserving great sympathy. Death can be a judgment (though it also can be an escape from evil times ahead—Isaiah 57:1-2). My guess is that in this case the family was subject to divine judgments.

The deaths placed a burden on Elimelech's wife, Naomi,

whose responsibility it became to remarry and provide sons for the widows of her two sons.[2] But Naomi was no longer capable of bearing children (Ruth 1:11-12). So she faced an impossible situation to which there was no solution. What was God saying to the family? Up until now I have assumed that Naomi was not a Baal worshiper but that her husband was. But was Naomi also? The story does not reveal.

Naomi is left without any grandchildren (Ruth 1). She has the responsibility of doing what she can to provide husbands for her daughters-in-law at a time when she can no longer bear children herself. Viewed in the light of the beliefs of the day, her situation is dire, and her longing for grandchildren is unmet. But God has had plans for her all along.

Are these facts relevant to us today? *Yes!*

We live surrounded by crime, by sexual infidelity even among Christians, by the threat of war, of financial collapse. (A surprising number of banks have failed—that is, some would have failed had not the government rescued them. *And more will fail.*) God's recent judgments can be seen in a long series of floods, famines, earthquakes, international disputes and wars. Yet we go on hoping that somehow matters will right themselves—because, like Naomi, we are in the dark. *We think we are in control, but we are not.*

The Contradictions of Judgment

Elimelech and his family had decided to escape the famine. They had chosen to move to Moab. How do we explain that while God's people suffered, the pagans around them were fine? It happens with surprising frequency. In Moab there were no emaciated cattle that had to be slaughtered, no dying infants, no elderly tottering on the brink of the grave, no hoarsely braying asses, no thirst. If anything, there was prosperity. It is an ancient problem—the wicked prosper and the righteous have a rough time.

But our view of matters is defective. God is the God of the whole earth. All nations and peoples belong to him. We do not know what his timing is in individual lives, far less in the lives of nations. God, not we ourselves, manages nations.

Israel was under judgment. You pay the price of being a chosen nation. Moab was neither a chosen nation nor—at least at that period—under judgment. Its time would come. Judgment *"begins* at the house of God." "For it is time for judgment to begin with the family of God; and if it begins with us, what will the outcome be for those who do not obey the gospel of God? And, 'If it is hard for the righteous to be saved, what will become of the ungodly and the sinner?' " (1 Peter 4:17-18).

Let us dread the judgment that is about to fall on the earth. Let us humble ourselves and repent and plead with God! We are in the same position as Elimelech's family seemed to be.

As Hope Returns

Yet there is always hope. It may not seem so at the time, but for the truly godly person there is no need to despair. The three deaths plus the absence of grandchildren were surely more than enough to make Naomi bitter, but I doubt these facts were the real cause of her bitterness. Death happens. It shocks us. We lose people who mean everything to us. The experience leaves us empty, alone. We weep and mourn, and there seems no end to our grief. But God deals with the living. Of the dead we have little knowledge. All our records are living records, having to do with living people, and people recover—usually—even from the loss of a husband and two sons.

God made us so that hope would return in the end, springing up unbidden to surprise us. Alexander Pope asserted, "Hope springs eternal in the human breast. / Man never is, but always to be blessed."

Hope deferred may indeed make the heart sick (Proverbs 13:12), but when the living have had time to let death's wounds heal, hope and joy begin to peep through the ground again. Desire springs up once more. Time will heal even the loss of dear ones.

What makes us bitter is not loss but *misplaced hopes and longings*. We had hoped, we had planned, and everything we had counted on turned to ashes. We tried extremely hard. Against all odds, we struggled endlessly. We mistakenly thought we had some control over life. But in the end, we failed. We could no longer go on fighting, for we grew weary and the fight seemed endless. Gradually we were worn down. In the end we despaired. And then we became bitter. We thought we could make it, but now we face the fact that we are not strong enough to cope, not good enough.

I do not know exactly what happened in Naomi's case, only that she became, by her own confession, a bitter woman. I do know that there was, as there always is, a cause for bitterness— Naomi's or anyone else's. God judges.

You will sow much seed in the field but you will harvest little, because locusts will devour it. You will plant vineyards and cultivate them but you will not drink the wine or gather the grapes, because worms will eat them. You will have olive trees throughout your country but you will not use the oil, because the olives will drop off. You will have sons and daughters but you will not keep them, because they will go into captivity. Swarms of locusts will take over all your trees and the crops of your land. (Deuteronomy 28:38-42)

It may seem strange that love lies behind judgment. C. S. Lewis once said that God shouts through pain. Behind all his judgments is a God of love, and his love is a passionate love.

The Pursuit

In the midst of Naomi's bitterness, perhaps after some years of being without her husband and sons, light begins to break on this deeply troubled woman. The first light-bearing crack in her bitterness appears. Remember, in those days people took God and the gods seriously.

When she heard in Moab that the LORD had come to the aid of his people by providing food for them, Naomi and her daughters-in-law prepared to return home from there. (1:6)

Even though Naomi thought the Lord was the source of her trouble, still she sees a glimmer of hope in returning to the land of her ancestors, the land promised by her God.

The difficulties which Naomi and Ruth face are still enormous. Naomi sees herself as barren, having passed the childbearing age. She has lost family and status. She feels her humiliation. Nothing remains for Naomi but to go home and face a lonely old age. Her house and land, still recognized as Elimelech's property, will subsequently be up for redemption (4:1-7). But God has better things in mind for both Ruth and Naomi.

The second sign of God's pursuit of Naomi comes in Ruth's decision to continue on with Naomi no matter what. Ruth, showing one degree of devotion more than Orpah, clings to her mother-in-law. She will not leave her. This clinging and this putting her mother-in-law's interests above her own remain consistent throughout the book. In the long run, and in the kindness of God, Ruth's actions benefit both herself and Naomi.

Naomi, the realist, begs Ruth to reconsider. She still tells Ruth to leave as Orpah already has. Perhaps she has no wish to be saddled with a daughter-in-law who might change her mind when it is too late to do so. But Ruth has thought the matter through in considerable detail. Clearly her mind is made up. Her words, mentioned earlier, are classic, well-known and powerful. They bear repeating here.

> Don't urge me to leave you or to turn back from you. Where
> you go I will go, and where you stay I will stay. Your people
> will be my people and your God my God. (1:16)

My heart leaps as I read them. Ruth is prepared to sacrifice both her gods and her friends. Her heart has experienced the pull of Israel's God, and that is enough for her. Who is this mysterious God who tugs at her? What has she learned from Naomi and her late husband? Has Naomi perhaps talked to her about the amazing God of Israel? Were Naomi's own words from years earlier now bearing fruit in Ruth, fruit that would in return begin to nourish Naomi herself so that she can feed on more than bitter roots?

Ruth's words should be the words of every Christian who knows that for all of us heaven will be a thoroughly different experience from personal relationships as we have found them on earth. In that sense we will find heaven as Ruth would find Israel—a foreign country, and yet home. But perhaps not "home" in the way we have always thought of it—a sort of warm, fuzzy, "homey" place! When we get there we will know, as we cannot know now, that we have come home. We are committed to something we cannot yet understand. We call going there "going home." We know not whereof we speak, but heaven will become home in a way we cannot now understand immediately when we arrive. It is we—not heaven—who will be changed.

Ruth's words have all the marks of an unshakable resolution.

They show her strength of conviction, her strong will and her willingness to submit. Naomi looks at the woman clinging to her and begins to see that something more powerful than she has yet encountered has happened to her daughter-in-law. Her urging ceases, and perhaps a fraction of bitterness leaves her. What has caused Ruth to say, "Where you die I will die, and there I will be buried. May the LORD deal with me, be it ever so severely, if anything but death separates you and me" (1:17)? Only the Spirit of God can awaken such unshakable resolutions.

In this way the Hound of Heaven pursues Naomi "with unhurrying chase, and unperturbed pace." The pursuit continues in the following chapters of Ruth as God continues to seek to win Naomi back. She thinks he is far from her and that she is far from him. Yet even when God seems farthest from us, he pursues. He does not give up.

2

Divine
Providence

*"I cried like a swift or thrush, I moaned like a mourning dove.
My eyes grew weak as I looked to the heavens. I am troubled;
O Lord, come to my aid!" But what can I say? He has spoken to me,
and he himself has done this. I will walk humbly all my years
because of this anguish of my soul. Lord, by such things men live;
and my spirit finds life in them too. You restored me to health
and let me live. (Isaiah 38:14-16)*

T he salvation/sanctification of Naomi and Ruth continues.
They meet with what appears to be, but is not, a coincidence. A
faithful Father controls things for them, the Spirit begins to show
them mercy, the Shepherd seeks them.

How Providence Works

Now Naomi had a relative on her husband's side, from the
clan of Elimelech, a man of standing, whose name was Boaz.
(Ruth 2:1)

From the way the verse above is worded, you might think you
were reading a fairy story. You could almost say, "It just so
happened that Naomi had a relative . . ." Were it not for the fact
that Scripture everywhere presents a God who is absolutely

sovereign, we would be inclined to view the whole story as a fairy tale. After all, books such as Ruth and Esther certainly read like fiction, and Jesus himself seemed to use fictitious situations in his parables in order to teach important lessons. But the book of Ruth is not fiction.

Boaz is "a man of standing." Whatever else the expression implies, we should note that the same expression is used of Jephthah in Judges 11:1 and is there translated as "a mighty warrior." (A comparable expression is used of Gideon.) Boaz is described as a relative of Naomi's late husband, Elimelech. Thus he is not related to Naomi except by marriage. But we are dealing with relationships more comparable to those in a clan or tribe, in which people provide for each other. Clearly Boaz held the respect of the community, perhaps by virtue of his wealth or his wisdom. A man of standing and a spiritual warrior, Boaz exemplifies the searching shepherd, tactfully and gently coming to the rescue of not one but two sheep.

The relationship between mother-in-law and daughter-in-law appears to have been an easy one, with give-and-take on both sides. Each understands that Naomi will have a certain authority in the relationship both because of her age and because of her position in the family. Respect for elders is a common feature of Middle Eastern cultures, and Ruth is no exception when it comes to her mother-in-law. In addition, Naomi is more traveled, and she knows her own country and its customs. Yet Naomi does not seem to be a particularly controlling woman. Ruth asks permission, and Naomi readily provides it.

> So Ruth the Moabitess said to Naomi, "Let me go to the fields and pick up the leftover grain behind anyone in whose eyes I find favor." (2:2)

Let her go? Must she have permission before doing anything?

Have I been mistaken in assuming the relationship is an easy, relaxed one? Does Naomi control Ruth's movements? No, but Naomi is older and knows the culture. Ruth is respectful. She acknowledges a degree of authority that would be perfectly appropriate under the circumstances. Therefore, her mother-in-law at once concurs: "Go ahead, my daughter" (2:2).

From this point on the story's wonder grows and grows. Ruth is not someone who does not know her own mind. After all, she had insisted against all Naomi's resistance that she would die where Naomi died and would worship Naomi's God. Grateful for Ruth's determined stance, grateful for someone who would stand with her on the long journey, Naomi must have felt a degree of relief. And on the journey that followed, neither seemed to have had the intention of dominating the other. God's judgments may have felt terrible to Naomi in Moab, but as the journey continued she would be very grateful for companionship—perhaps even suspect that God is not harsh but has to be severe in judgment.

Once we grasp the wonder of a God who is absolutely sovereign yet who is deeply concerned about the welfare of ordinary men and women, issues like his judgments become easier to understand. Instead of our frantic and distressed "Why, Lord, *why?*" we may begin with bewilderment, and before long we progress to the point when we marvel at his ways.

God is both sovereign and personal. He loves, and his love is a tender yet holy love. This combination makes him a little scary to approach, but we are exhorted to boldness as we do so.

Ruth's Efforts

As Ruth set out in search of work, she probably looked with a keen eye for a field where the poor were welcomed. Naomi may have told her of the practice in Israel that made some provision for the poor. Ruth would begin as a *gleaner,* someone who gathered grain left behind by the reapers. According to Old Testament law, the poor were allowed to harvest such remains from fields they did not work. "When you reap the harvest of your land, do not reap to the very edges of your field or gather the gleanings of your harvest. Do not go over your vineyard a second time or pick up the grapes that have fallen. Leave them for the poor and the alien. I am the LORD your God" (Leviticus 19:9-10). Gleaning was an old custom, having its roots in kindly Old Testament practice, originating in God's mercy to the poor.

Ruth might try to size up the situation among the workers and the gleaners alike, going from field to field to see what the prospects might be in each. Were the workers content, or were they surly? Were overseers cruel or gentle? My feeling about Ruth is that in spite of her determination to come to Israel and to know Israel's God, she would be cautious in her first ventures into the community. You approach matters cautiously when you are in a new country. I know. I've been in many countries, and I'm not always sure how to relate to the people, even the Christians.

Of course, I could be wrong about Ruth. She may not have had the time to do all this. She might have gone directly to the nearest field to glean. Because the biblical text is condensed, we are not told exactly what Ruth's actions are. She has yet to learn confidence in the God of Israel, though doubtless that confidence will come. For now she may have used her common sense and the caution anyone in a new situation or country exercises.

So when Ruth says to Naomi, perhaps after such a cautious survey of the fields where people are working on the barley harvest, "Let me go to the fields and pick up the leftover grain behind anyone in whose eyes I find favor," the succession of events that follow is in God's hands. Neither woman has the least suspicion of how matters will end.

Is it always so? Yes, especially when we want to please God. Even when we do not care about pleasing him in the least, he may take charge of our lives anyway and cause our hearts to seek until we find him. In Romans 9 Paul makes a case for this divine providence. Specifically, he cites the example of God's choice of Jacob over his brother Esau.

Not only that, but Rebekah's children had one and the same father, our father Isaac. *Yet, before the twins were born or had done anything good or bad—in order that God's purpose in election might stand:* not by works but by him who calls—she was told, "The older will serve the younger." Just as it is written: "Jacob I loved, but Esau I hated." What then shall we say? Is God unjust? Not at all! (Romans 9:10-14)

Likewise, God's hand in Ruth's endeavor becomes evident early on. She chooses a field in which to work. She has no idea of the course of events that will so profoundly affect her future. She has simply come to glean what she can to provide for herself and Naomi.

Then comes the feeling of an unfolding fairy tale.

As it turned out, [Ruth] found herself working in a field belonging to Boaz. (2:3)

As it turned out? Could it have turned out otherwise? This phrase also implies that *Ruth did not know about Boaz* or did not understand the custom of kinsman-redeemers. We are dealing with no fairy story but with God's own plot, his plan. God controls all things, working circumstances together on behalf of those who love him.

Can you imagine a society today where this would happen?

God is kind. In Leviticus 19:1 he asserts that he is the Lord of Israel. As the Lord, the Yahweh, of Israel, he commands that not all the grapes in vineyards are to be gleaned and that corners of unscythed wheat (or barley) are to be left for the poor and the aliens. One of the tasks the church faces is to work toward a similar society, where the poor can labor so that they really earn their bread. God's provisional system did not allow for people who never worked. Nor did it allow slavery in the sense of exhausting oneself to keep body and soul together. The system proved better than the welfare system of any country in today's world, because gleaning demanded work. The problems welfare has created affect all westernized countries today.

The God of Boaz
While Ruth works in the field, Boaz arrives from Bethlehem. God has been working on Boaz for a long time. He is a God who transforms the character of every person who is willing to go along with the process, and Boaz was a part of his saving, sanctifying work. It may not always feel as though he is helping. Sometimes God seems to be obstructing us rather than helping us to be holy. But always when he obstructs, it is better that we be obstructed.

Personally I do not like the process of sanctification, or should I say sanctification as an experience. There are parts of it I enjoy. For instance, I have found that when God convicts me of sin, he never seems to do it like the Accuser does. Somehow it comes across as a kind of relief. The response is more like *Oh, I see now what was bothering me!* However, it is not always like that. The sins I most resist are the sins I do not want to know about; then the Lord's methods are sometimes a little rougher.

Was the process like this for Boaz? How has he turned out so far? He seems to be a courteous employer whose custom it is to greet his workers. "The LORD be with you!" he calls, and "The LORD bless you!" the reply comes back (2:4). Simple stuff. But courtesy is a good beginning. Of course, the courtesy can be meaningless and can even cover avarice and cunning. But normally when it does, the reply is a surly, muttered reply. Employees can spot cunning and avaricious employers.

Boaz seems also to be observant. He notices Ruth's presence immediately, picking her out from harvesters, servant girls and gleaners. "Whose young woman is that?" (2:5). Immediately he seeks to know about this new worker.

"She is the Moabitess who came back from Moab with Naomi," says his foreman (2:6). The man goes on to explain that she had asked courteously to be allowed to glean among the sheaves behind the harvesters. Evidently the foreman had given her leave. He tells Boaz that she has worked steadily picking up leftover grain, except for a short rest (2:7). Thus Ruth has not only clung and gone on clinging protectively to Naomi but has volunteered to work, knowing what she might face, and has so far worked hard and well. She meant it when she said that only death would separate her from Naomi. She is faithful to those she loves.

Immediately Boaz goes to her, and we see more of what God has done in him over the years. "My daughter, listen to me," he tells her. "Don't go and glean in another field and don't go away from here" (2:8). Boaz knows she is Naomi's daughter-in-law. Why does he address her as "my daughter"? Is that a conventional way of addressing her, or does it imply special concern? Why does he go on to exhort her, "Listen to me . . ."?

Let me deal with the second question first. Boaz's instruction to listen emphasizes that he wants her to pay careful attention. Why? So far as we know, there is no evidence of his being attracted to Ruth as a woman. Yet he exhorts her not to go to any other field. He knows of her goodness to Naomi. Clearly he wants to help Ruth and Naomi.

To address Ruth as "my daughter" is spoken of by commentators as pointing to a disparity in their ages, another sign, perhaps, that no sexual attraction could be very strong at that early stage. Sensual old men may eye any woman lasciviously, but Boaz is not a sensual old man. His community standing argues against this. Uppermost in his mind is simple kindness. She is a Gentile foreigner and in special need of care. He will do what he can for her because he has God's heart in him.

Boaz continues, "Stay here with my servant girls" (2:8). What does this mean? Let me quote Leon Morris in his commentary on Ruth: "[Boaz] now gives her a direction to remain with his maidservants. This apparently indicates some sort of status in Boaz' household."[1] Boaz is simply showing kindness to a gleaner and is clearly impressed and touched by the kindness a Gentile and a foreigner has shown to Naomi, his relative.

Though Ruth knows little or nothing of the God who has been pulling her, something of this man's integrity is probably getting through to her. Boaz continues,

Watch the field where the men are harvesting, and follow along after the girls. I have told the men not to touch you. And whenever you are thirsty, go and get a drink from the water jars the men have filled. (2:9)

Boaz allows Ruth to follow after the girls who are binding the sheaves. Morris has a long note at this point which is worth quoting in full.

One can imagine that the enthusiasm of the gleaners would cause them to encroach on the legitimate property of the owners of the crops unless they were checked, and that accordingly the reapers might repulse, by force, if necessary, any who came too near before the owners were through. Ruth would know this and keep her distance. Boaz' instruction to Ruth enabled her to work close to the reapers in a position specially favorable for gleaning.[2]

Boaz knows what it is like to work under a burning sun. He is making her job easier for her by placing her in such a good position to glean and by offering her water when she needs it.

Boaz is also protecting her. Once again, Leon Morris helps me. He wrote long before *sexual harassment* became a buzzword. Yet given our own age in which we are tripping over ourselves to avoid the very appearance of sexual harassment, he sees how modern folly was avoided long ago in Ruth's day. Morris says, "But this very position (close to the reapers) exposed her to the possibility of rude jests and even mishandling from the workmen. [Boaz] now tells her that he has guarded against this by giving instructions to the reapers that they were to leave her alone."[3] Boaz knows the men he employs, knows how some of them look at this woman and knows what could happen to her. So he assures her that he has already taken the trouble to speak to the men, warning them against trying to approach or molest her (2:9).

Ruth is overwhelmed and grateful. She bows to the ground, crying,

"Why have I found such favor in your eyes that you notice me—a foreigner?"

Boaz replied, "I've been told all about what you have done for your mother-in-law since the death of your husband—how you left your father and mother and your homeland and came to live with a people you did not know before. May the LORD repay you for what you have done. May you be richly rewarded by the LORD, the God of Israel, under whose wings you have come to take refuge." (2:10-12)

But Ruth does not know the depth of God's working, even though she must have been stunned by such kindness. We know that everything that has happened to her was part of a plan that antedated the creation of the world (Romans 1:20; Ephesians 1:4). We also know what happened to her descendants, but she knows nothing of this. She does not even know what kind of a God it is under whose wings she has taken refuge, or why she feels so attracted to Yahweh, Israel's God. God has chosen her, and she is drawn to a destiny without knowing it.

Is this fatalism? No! Certainly not!

Two things distinguish what I have said from fatalism. First, fatalism is a cruel doctrine, and the Judeo-Christian beliefs are the product of a God of love. Second, that love is never forced on us. We are wonderfully, deeply loved, and we have a choice. We may refuse it. To choose or to reject is a prerogative God gave us. He selects, he chooses—this is how our salvation begins. It is pure grace, pure mercy. But thereafter we still have a choice. My God is no rapist and will never force his love and kindness on an unwilling victim. I also know that redemption is enough for all the world. There is nothing limited about the death of Christ.

The Father is a *masculine* (not a male) member of the Trinity. Masculine implies someone who is inclined to initiate. Among other things, he initiates love. A true Christian may refuse his love. The Holy Spirit is gentle. He woos, but his wooing can be scorned. In the incredible mercy of a God of love, God has chosen to limit himself. He knows he is sovereign, and he suffers no sense of inferiority. Before whom would he be inferior? He chooses freely to accept, and as freely to reject those who will not heed his pleading but who fill their cup of iniquity full. We are free to refuse, but—and at this point I perceive a mystery— we who have accepted have always been chosen. We seem to have no choice whatever to accept, even though it may appear to us that we chose to accept God. The interactions of human beings with divine love are highly mysterious.

Ruth Arrives Home

When Ruth goes home to Naomi that night, perhaps hurrying a little in her eagerness (as well as she can with the burden of grain she carries), she still knows nothing about the special place Boaz has in their life. So she talks to Naomi about her day. Quite obviously she would have been excited and, whether loquacious or not, would have a lot to tell. Things had gone extraordinarily well. She tells Naomi enthusiastically, "The name of the man I worked with today is Boaz" (2:19).

"The LORD bless him!" Naomi says to her daughter-in-law. And then Naomi begins to marvel at God's blessing: "He has not stopped showing his kindness to the living and the dead" (2:20).

Here we see Naomi take another step away from her bitter-ness. Something is happening in her innermost being. She is becoming dimly aware of a God who cares—perhaps who cares for her personally. The Shepherd has caught sight of her and is moving toward her.

Naomi adds, "That man is our close relative; he is one of our kinsman-redeemers" (2:20).

In ancient Israel each member of a family or clan was obli-gated to provide for their poor relations. A kinsman-redeemer was responsible to buy back property that had been sold by a relative in time of severe need. This responsibility could extend to providing the destitute relative with an heir through marriage. Perhaps Naomi explains to Ruth at this point what a kinsman-redeemer is.

Then Ruth the Moabitess said, "He even said to me, 'Stay with my workers until they finish harvesting all my grain.'" (2:21) Boaz's suggestion is quite in line with Naomi's own fears for her daughter-in-law's safety. Naomi naturally feels a deep affection for Ruth and wants her protected. In addition, Ruth is the breadwinner, and neither can afford to see her hurt. So Naomi tells Ruth,

It will be good for you, my daughter, to go with his girls, because in someone else's field you might be harmed. (2:22) Matters settle easily for a while. Harvest is an especially busy period for farms. It can also be a time of rejoicing and celebration when the harvest is plentiful. Naomi and Ruth are probably part of the celebration that marked the end of harvest, and the offerings would follow. Their first experiences in Bethlehem prove fortunate.

Time is full during first the barley harvest, then, hard on its heels, the wheat harvest. Ruth stays close to Boaz's servant girls during the day, drinking her fill from the water jars, probably falling into a profound slumber when she gets home at night. But Naomi's mind begins to form a plan. Profound gratitude for Ruth's company and hard work gradually begins to bear fruit in Naomi's heart.

Slowly their store of grain increases. And Naomi's bitterness decreases more and more as she sees the provision of the Almighty for the two of them. She has much of the day to think, and her thoughts revolve around Boaz and Ruth. What steps should she take? Does she pray to Yahweh? Her subsequent advice certainly reflects the mind of God. The story actually tells us little about the spiritual progress in Naomi's heart. Yet of one thing I am sure: wittingly or unwittingly, Naomi is directed by God in all her counsel to Ruth. As we shall see in the next chapter, she makes her move as the harvest draws to its close.

And whether Naomi is conscious of the fact or not, she thinks along the lines that God wants her to. The God whom she did not know as Father had foreseen all things before time existed, knew what would happen and had caused it to happen. The Father was waiting for her, looking eagerly from the rooftop.

3

Submission

As God both foresaw and arranged the lives of Naomi and Ruth, he had already determined the contents of a conversation to come. The conversation would be spoken quietly so as not to awaken persons sleeping nearby. There would also be a further act of great kindness, again, doubtless carried out without unnecessary noise. The conversation and the act of kindness would both take place during the stillness of the night at a certain threshing floor not far from Bethlehem.

Naomi's Hope

The story of the two women continues to approach a climax. The shepherd who searches for his two sheep will soon find them. He loves all, even though he chooses some. God has pursued not only Naomi but also Ruth.

Naomi never forgets her obligation to Ruth, who has stuck with her on the long journey, being willing to live with her, worship with her and die with her. It is clear that whenever Naomi thinks of Ruth, she does so fondly, even tenderly. This is significant. So long as you remain bitter, you think only of yourself. But Naomi has begun to think of Ruth. In New Testament language, she is becoming sanctified.

But how can she "fix Ruth up"? How can she find a permanent home for her daughter-in-law—a place in the community where she will be respected? The more Naomi ponders the possibilities, the more often she thinks of Boaz. Perhaps she even prays about the matter.

What is his situation? Naomi probably asks and likely learns a lot of things about him that Bible scholars of today no longer know, for we are remote from what actually happened. For instance, was he married? A widower? Most likely he was either single or a widower.

Later we learn that Ruth does not run after the "younger" men (3:10); this implies that Boaz is older than she by some years. So if I were to guess, I would opt for his being a widower who had loved his wife dearly and passionately but with sorrow had buried her some years previously, mourning and later recovering. His character suggests this. But I could be quite wrong, and I suppose it is foolish of me to speculate. At any rate, we see him presently as a courteous, kindly man, who clearly thinks of others every bit as much as he thinks of himself.

Ruth's Submission

Does Naomi think that Boaz is the only kinsman-redeemer? No, as she said earlier, "[Boaz] is one of our kinsman-redeemers" (2:20). There are others. But she thinks only of Boaz, that he will make an excellent husband for Ruth. Naomi is a *matchmaker!*

Matchmaking dies hard among us, and provided it is not too intrusive, it can be a useful activity. A song in the musical *Fiddler on the Roof* even celebrates matchmaking as a respectable profession. Providing a husband for Ruth has been on Naomi's mind since before they left Moab (1:11). Naomi must have been thinking about Boaz and Ruth along these lines from the moment that Ruth had told her whose field she had selected.

A conversation between Naomi and Ruth shows that matchmaking was a far more serious business then than now. Naomi delicately broaches the subject one day:

My daughter, should I not try to find a home for you, where you will be well provided for? (3:1)

Is there a pause? Does Ruth respond, or does she look at her mother-in-law with a beating heart? She realizes that she does not know enough of the ways of the culture she has inherited to venture on her own. The culture has a number of features similar to the one she so firmly abandoned, but it has many others as well that arose from God's revelation to Abraham and to Moses, and she has to be careful. If she has any feelings for Boaz, she does not reveal them. In any case, people were far more practical about marriage then than people now.

Ruth is interested in the God of Israel—she has to be if she is willing to make him her God. As far as she can tell, he is both stern and kind. Naomi has spoken much about him to her, and even if Naomi has been somewhat negative in the way she sees him, that same God is drawing Ruth to himself. This is an important spiritual reality behind the whole story.

Naomi's plan (and God's) centers on the winnowing of the barley harvest. Once all the grain was gathered, workers take it to a threshing floor (often an exposed platform that could take advantage of the wind), where the barley will be thrown into the air so the lighter chaff can blow away and the remaining grain fall back to the floor. This is hard work, but there is also a celebratory atmosphere of eating and drinking as the final stage of the harvest is completed.

Naomi continues her instructions to Ruth:

Wash and perfume yourself, and put on your best clothes. Then go down to the threshing floor, but don't let him know you are there until he has finished eating and drinking. When he lies down, note the place where he is lying. (3:3-4)

Wow! Really, isn't that going too far, too fast?

Not really. The exercise is not one of exciting Boaz's passions so much as testing his kindness, his willingness to help. It is rooted in the tradition of the kinsman-redeemer. Boaz can do something Naomi cannot; he can redeem (apart from his ability to redeem debts) and rectify Ruth's widowhood, perhaps even giving her the very children that Naomi's son had not been able to. He can thus secure her line and also the line of Elimelech, Naomi's late husband.

God himself is interested; all this time, he is looking on. He is arranging matters far beyond what Naomi can see and is directing Naomi's thoughts. Those thoughts, even though she might not know it, are God's thoughts.

The attraction of a woman to a man (or of a man to a woman) is not unimportant or even wrong. Ruth is to wash, to wear perfume and to dress nicely. But the physical attraction is secondary to the main purpose of awakening a responsible kindness in Boaz. God had in mind something more important than the immediate events; he had in mind the redemptive antecedents of his Son. Though Jesus came from human descendants, we know that he was free from all sin. Nevertheless, God chose the line by which his own Son would come into the world with great care.

Wonderfully, Ruth chooses to submit herself to Naomi's directions. Since the winnowing was often for men only, Ruth would need to be careful. In addition, Naomi asks Ruth to submit to whatever Boaz might instruct (3:4). Ruth's original commitment to Naomi has stood firm. She recognizes the wisdom, trusts her mother-in-law's judgment and does exactly as she has instructed. "I will do whatever you say," she tells Naomi (3:5).

Naomi emphasizes, "He will tell you what to do." How well does Naomi know Boaz? She probably has made discreet inquiries about him. She has likely observed him closely since her recent arrival. She seems to size up the situation very well. Perhaps she prays, seeking divine guidance. But Ruth, in accordance with the instructions she receives, will discreetly watch the place Boaz lies down in good spirits after he finishes eating and drinking.

Here I pause to consider an issue on which Christians differ, that of alcohol. In biblical times, God's people drank wine and were, if not encouraged to drink it, certainly given instructions in how and when to drink (see Deuteronomy 14:26). The contented feeling you get when you have eaten and drunk wine is what Boaz experienced.

There are Christians who do not drink. And this is an appropriate decision for many. Some of them, however, may feel virtuous about what they *do not do,* adding to the wall between Christians and non-Christians and possibly making them self-righteous. Those Christians who do drink occasionally may feel their own sense of superiority of being above legalistic constraints. Such pride also stinks in the nostrils of God.

The problem created by alcoholism, of course, is enormous

and not to be taken lightly. It existed in the days of Moses and is condemned as drunkenness in Scripture. I occasionally enjoy a glass of wine with my evening meal. I did so tonight. After a good meal and a glass of wine, you feel content. If you want to, you can sleep. But tonight I chose to write instead. I can therefore appreciate Boaz's contented frame of mind. I enjoy that same mood as I write.

I was brought up in England, where Christians have a quite different attitude toward alcohol than many in North America. In fact, throughout Europe and many other parts of the world conservative Christians do not observe an absolute prohibition against alcohol nor see such mandates in Scripture, though they do recognize that the Bible clearly condemns its abuse.

There was a time, however, when the more I drank, the more I didn't want to stop. Once I got drunk after visiting my mother's grave. Then one day, probably because my wife did not hesitate to point out what was happening, I realized I must quit. After some thought and prayer I did so.

Christians should not be alcoholics, but then, many of us have ancestors who were alcoholics. Genetic studies of alcoholism make clear this propensity in some families. Some people can handle alcohol in limited amounts, while other people cannot. Yet God has ways of healing us forever, and I am grateful that he chose to intervene and deliver me.

Alcoholics and sex addicts alike can be self-deceived and tend to deceive others. We are all corrupt and corruptible. More than this, we are all worshipers of the ancient gods (or of fallen angelic beings). Earlier I suggested that sex was a gift that God gave us. Did you nod your head? If you did, look at the mess that even Christians are making of sex! So I ask, Why do the good gifts that God gave to humanity become subject to abuse? Being sinners, we abuse them in a world that we ourselves in our ancestors gave to Satan's power.

Alcoholism is widespread among believers in Jesus Christ. So is sexual sin. Many Christians are involved in homosexuality, child molestation, adultery and premarital sex. Usually they convince themselves that it is okay but hide it from the church, because "some Christians would not understand." Or else they visit a psychologist or a psychiatrist to look for help.

If we suggest that we all quit alcohol, we might also suggest the same thing about sex. The human race could end pretty quickly that way. Actually, alcohol within biblical restrictions can be just as legitimate as sex within biblical limits. If we are outside the limits, we must ask God to deliver us as we repent of our sin, reject Satan's power in our lives and change our ways.

"He Will Tell You What to Do"

Boaz likely gives little thought to choosing a place on the threshing floor; he certainly is unaware that someone is watching him carefully. As he makes his way to privacy beyond the mountain of grain, Ruth notes his movements.

Ruth carefully conceals her presence from him, waiting for the right moment to fulfill Naomi's instructions. Eventually the threshing floor quiets down. Perhaps one or two merrymakers continue to chatter and laugh for a while, but then all subsides. Ruth waits until all is quite still, then steals quietly to lie at Boaz's feet, which she carefully uncovers according to Naomi's instructions.

This action was not intended to be immoral but to signify a formal request for marriage. Lying at his feet was a position indicating submission. And Ruth curls up quietly at his feet and waits. What will happen? Will he reject the request? Will he send her away? There is the possibility of success in the plan, but there is also the danger of failure and dashed hopes.

When I think of Ruth, and of following these potentially dangerous instructions carefully, I think also of Mary, the mother of our Lord, who followed the similarly alarming angelic instructions. She, like Ruth, waited, trusting and willing to do God's will. When the angel Gabriel appeared to her, she was not only startled but afraid. She was even more bewildered when he gave her the news he brought.

> But the angel said to her, "Do not be afraid, Mary, you have found favor with God. You will be with child and give birth to a son, and you are to give him the name Jesus. He will be great and will be called the Son of the Most High. The Lord God will give him the throne of his father David, and he will reign over the house of Jacob forever; his kingdom will never end." (Luke 1:30-33)

It is hardly surprising that Mary would be afraid, and perhaps badly shaken. We live in a day when angelic appearances are increasing. They can be both awesome and frightening. But Mary knew perfectly well that babies only come one way. Hesitantly she mentioned her virginity. "How will this be," Mary asked the angel, "since I am a virgin?" And at that point the angel gave her news that—at least when I think of modern, scientific people—was *way* more startling than what we would expect.

Angels are startling enough, but supernatural pregnancies are another matter altogether. The angel answered, "The Holy Spirit will come upon you, and the power of the Most High will overshadow you. So the holy one to be born will be called the Son of God" (Luke 1:35). Supernatural pregnancies are unique.

Yes, angelic experiences can shake us. One Sunday during the worship in a Vineyard church, my wife Lorrie said, "John, there's a great big bird in here!" Puzzled, she started to turn around to try to see where it was. After a minute or so she turned a bewildered face to me and whispered, "I can feel the draft from its wings, but I can't see anything!" Personally, I don't believe angels have wings, but in any case I saw nothing and felt nothing. I suppose God deals with us according to the pictures in our minds, and many people picture winged angels.

At the time, I was on the thirty-seventh day of a forty-day fast. It was a fast God had commanded me to engage in, a fast he had called "*my* fast!" I am not altogether clear what he meant by that, but I took it that the fast bore some relationship to the fast Jesus engaged in before his ministry. At any rate, I was driven to it and only engaged in it because I was told to.

On one particular Sunday I was due to preach. As I made my tottery way (being weak after so long a fast on water alone) down the steps toward the platform, I was suddenly overwhelmed by enormous physical strength that transformed me, reverberating powerfully inside my body. A heavy steel stool had been placed on the stage of the school theater where we were meeting. As I got to the stage, a little showily, I seized the stool low down by the leg, raised it in the air and put it aside. My upper body is weak—and I could not do that normally, even when I was not fasting.

I was profoundly grateful to God for his help in sending what I believe was an angel of strength. It reminded me that angels came to him at that point in his fast, and I have believed in their reality much more since that time. I fasted as God instructed me to, even though I didn't know all the reasons why, what dangers it might bring me or all that it would mean.

Likewise God called Ruth through Naomi and Mary through Gabriel to do his bidding even when they did not fully understand all that would come from these actions. In all these cases, God was glorified in ways we could not have imagined. From such simple obedience can come great gain for his kingdom.

God's Voice

As mentioned above, Ruth must follow one last instruction from Naomi. After Ruth is lying at Boaz's feet, she is to do what Boaz tells her to do (3:4). Behind all the instructions that Naomi has given and those that Boaz would give, another voice has been speaking and directing, whether Naomi and Boaz realize it or not. A sovereign God has been directing every event. God desires to speak to all his people. He desires to address every one of us. The Father has been waiting.

I know there is an interaction between human will and God's sovereign will. God does not make a practice of violating and crushing human volition. Usually we seem to have a choice in how we respond to his prompting. The whole business is mysterious, and we shall not fully understand it until a coming day.

The apostle Paul strongly emphasizes our need to bow to God's sovereign will. When Paul chose his own way God made him physically blind in order to shake him into seeing reality (Acts 9:1-17). *Submission to the will of God is of great importance, and we cannot obey and submit unless we learn to hear his speech.*

God may take certain men and women by the scruff of the neck and show them rather forcefully that their ideas are not worth a hill of beans. He "falls on" them, shakes them into an awareness of his might and power. But even so, if they want to resist God, he will never crush them to *make* them understand.

Paul eventually chose deliberately to hear the voice of the Holy Spirit and to submit to it. In the Old Testament it was always

"The Lord said . . ." But in the New it becomes "The Holy Spirit said . . ." Did those in the New Testament church not have the Old Testament Scripture? Of course they did, and they paid heed to what it said more than we do ourselves today. But following Christ, they knew God in three persons. We need Scripture more than we ever did. But we also need the voice of the Spirit. Always that voice will be consistent with biblical principles. The two—Scripture and the Spirit's voice—will never be in conflict, and it is vital that we get to know Scripture better and better.

But think for a minute. Do you want to enjoy fellowship with God? In Acts 16:9-10 we read of Paul having a vision of a man from Macedonia calling for help. At once he gathers that God wants him and his team to go there. He obeys. You say, "The Scripture is enough for me. I do not need anything more!" Really? Where does Scripture itself tell Paul to go to Macedonia and preach? Where else could Paul have gone to get that sort of prompting? Either we write Paul off as crazy, or we had better start to learn to listen to God's voice. And—this is where the risk and the fear come in—we had better start submitting to that voice and obeying, in exactly the same way as Ruth submitted to Naomi and Boaz, and Paul submitted to the call from Macedonia.

We will never win some internal arguments because they come from the Accuser of the brethren, who starts to play games with us and accuse us. Both accusatory thoughts and self-glorifying thoughts come from the same source—darkness. Other thoughts will be reminders of God's kindness to us, of his goodness in general. Those are the kinds of thoughts God sends. But now and again he will say something equivalent to Paul's vision, and that may scare us a bit. "Is that really *you*, Lord?"

We should be very cautious about telling people what to do. We should likewise be very cautious when we think God is telling us to go somewhere or do something. It could be God. Or it could be Satan, and Satan is very good at fooling people. *So beg God to give you confirmation,* either from the Scripture or from someone else. Never try to twist Scripture to make it mean something it doesn't. God is always ready to help, and Satan gives up usually when you call out to God in fear.

At Boaz's Feet

It is hardly comfortable to sleep with your sandals or shoes on, though it can be done. Boaz may have been feeling so contented that he ignored the discomfort. It may be that Ruth took his sandals off as a way to uncover his feet. Perhaps uncovering his feet would rouse him when he got cold, allowing her to present her petition. Would Ruth sleep much? I tend to doubt it, and certainly when "something startled" Boaz, any sleep she had enjoyed would be over. What is it that has awakened Boaz? What startles him?

Whatever awoke him is a bit of a puzzle. I know that when something startles me in my sleep, I sit up immediately. So perhaps both of them sat up. The word used in the NIV is *startled.* In the King James it is *afraid.* Leon Morris says,

> The original meaning of the word is "tremble" and it has been suggested that Boaz trembled on account of the cold, his feet being uncovered. This cannot completely be ruled out, but the verb more commonly means "to be afraid" and it seems better to think that Boaz experienced a moment of terror on being woken suddenly.[2]

I am inclined to believe that the whole matter of Ruth's approach and her uncovering the feet of Boaz was as I had suggested. In this I differ a little from some commentaries, including Morris. At any rate, whatever the succession of events, by the time he saw a woman at his feet Boaz would certainly be startled.

"Who are you?" he asked.

"I am your servant Ruth," she said. "Spread the corner of your garment over me since you are a kinsman-redeemer." (3:9)

Boaz understands at that point. He comes from a world where kinsman-redeemers have a place. He understands what she has done, and why. What is more, he is moved and pleased—because she is kind enough to ask him to act as a kinsman-redeemer.

"The LORD bless you, my daughter," he replied. "This kindness is greater than that which you showed earlier." (3:10)

Kindness that Ruth showed him earlier? Is he referring to Ruth's kindness to Naomi—seeing it as a kindness to himself? Or is he referring to her coming to his field, not realizing that she has come guided only by Yahweh? Whichever it was, he is wonderfully aware of kindnesses done to him in situations where he had himself been expressing kindness. We need more men like him in the church. And Boaz continues to be kind, seeing as a kindness her very request, even her choice of him as an older man. He continues,

You have not run after the younger men, whether rich or poor. (3:10)

Is there the beginning of love here? Perhaps not. Remember the practicality of the whole business of marriage in that day. But at least there is very great kindness and an utter willingness to act as kinsman-redeemer to the best of his ability. Evidently Boaz is not impotent, and his potency will come in useful if Ruth is to bear children. Boaz says,

And now, my daughter, don't be afraid. I will do for you all
you ask. All my fellow townsmen know that you are a woman
of noble character. Although it is true that I am near of kin,
there is a kinsman-redeemer nearer than I. Stay here for the
night, and in the morning if he wants to redeem, good; let him
redeem. But if he is not willing, as surely as the LORD lives I
will do it. Lie here until morning. (3:11-14)

I am sure that at that point Boaz covers her with the corner of
his garment, signifying that whatever is to take place in the
morning, Ruth will no longer be a widow. He will certainly
guarantee his own side of a kinsman-redeemer's duty and is
determined to play his cards expertly with his fellow kinsman-
redeemer. As is so often the case, men have a better idea of the
way a man thinks, just as women can more easily tell what
women think.

I doubt that Ruth could go back to sleep. Her future was
secure. The God in whom she had placed her trust had shown
her he was concerned about her. Has the Father of us all begun
to run toward her as he ran in the parable of Luke 15? I suspect
that the wonder of all that has happened keeps her eyes wide
open for the remainder of the night.

Before Dawn Breaks
Just before the break of dawn, "before anyone could be recognized," Boaz says to Ruth, "Don't let it be known that a woman
came to the threshing floor" (3:14). Why the caution? Evidently
women did not sleep at the threshing floor, which was either an
all-male location from the start or one from which the women
retired before the night. Why, then, is he so concerned? Is he
worried about his reputation? I believe it would be consistent
with his kindness for him to think about Ruth's reputation rather

than his own. He is an older man. But he evidently has also been thinking of the coming negotiations with his fellow kinsman-redeemer.

Again Boaz does a great kindness, once more going significantly beyond the laws in Leviticus, as he has done previously (see 2:14). In so doing, he acts as the shepherd looking for the sheep and the Father waiting with longing for the son's return. His act reflects the Savior's own.

"Bring me the shawl you are wearing," he says (3:15). If it was a woolen shawl it would probably not be wrinkled, but it would have picked up bits and pieces of grain and chaff from the threshing floor. And while their sleep at the threshing floor was clearly chaste, the speckled appearance of her shawl could indicate otherwise to those she would meet. But Boaz has a plan to protect Ruth's reputation. Into the shawl she holds out, he pours six measures of barley. Now there will be no reason for others to question her appearance. She is carrying grain.

Then immediately he makes for the city gates, for he has important personal business to attend to there. He has to confront his fellow kinsman-redeemer.

When Ruth returns home, Naomi asks, "How did it go?" (3:16). Questions of this sort have been asked for centuries. Both women are excited, and an eager question-and-answer period would follow. Ruth cannot wait to tell everything that happened. If ever there were a blow-by-blow description, this one would be it!

Ruth tells the story, adding, "He gave me these six measures of barley, saying, 'Don't go back to your mother-in-law empty-handed'" (3:17). Naomi then confirms my suspicion that she has sized up Boaz to a T. Clearly she knows him well, whether from her own inquiries or not, for she says, "Wait, my daughter, until you find out what happens. *For the man will not rest until the matter is settled today"* (3:18). She knows he is a man of action who will carry out his mission as God intended.

4

The Gospel &
the Book of Ruth

*The truth is not in the middle, and not in one extreme
but in both extremes. (Charles Simeon)*

Charles Simeon served God diligently in an Anglican church in Cambridge in the late 1700s and early 1800s. Many people see him as the forefather of the Inter-Varsity movement in Great Britain.

Simeon believed that balanced Christianity did not entail taking a middle-of-the-road position but in emphasizing both ends of a spectrum. So he happily wrote of a "High Calvinist" one day and a "Low Arminian" the next. He meant that he fully believed that God was sovereign, but that a sovereign God who had saved him had attached certain commandments and conditions to his sovereign power to keep him. It was up to him to love God and to go on trusting his promises, such as Romans 8:28, "And we know that in all things God works for the good of *those who love him,* who have been *called according to his purpose."*

Called according to his purpose? We are called when we are truly converted, when regeneration has really taken place. Those who love him? Love and delight are awakened at this point. We delight in him, embrace him. Both the call and the love constitute the conditions of the promise—conditions of a genuine work of grace in our hearts. Both the love and the call are not conditions to be fulfilled so much as evidences of the reality and truth of God's call. When God calls, love and faith result.

This was Naomi's experience, but not right away. At the beginning of the book of Ruth, Naomi saw her life as a tragedy rather than as a preparation for God's blessing. Even in Ruth 3 she is still a very bitter woman, totally misunderstanding God's blessed and blessing purposes for her own life.

God never stops confusing us in this same way. At this point in my life I am totally bewildered! The further I go, my ignorance of the gospel message becomes plainer and plainer to me personally. God works mysteriously to bring good from otherwise bad events. The greatest good in Naomi's story is revealed in the last verses of the last chapter of the book of Ruth, a good she could hardly have ever imagined.

Old Testament Saints

Boaz is what used to be called an "Old Testament saint," or one who, before Christ came into the world, had already embraced his salvation. Like Job, he could cry, "I know that my Redeemer lives, and that in the end he will stand upon the earth" (Job 19:25).

How do we know that Boaz is an Old Testament saint? We know by two facts. First, he is presented to us as one whose actions pleased God. He is a model kinsman-redeemer. Second, he displays a distinctly Christlike character. The stamp of salvation is on him. He is like Mary Magdalene in the New Testament, who by her love and gratitude clearly shows that her repentance is the genuine kind (Luke 7:36-50). The more we know about Boaz the man, the more his Christlikeness becomes evident. His willingness to act as kinsman-redeemer (Ruth 2—3) and his patent honesty in dealing with his fellow kinsman-redeemer (as we will soon see in examining Ruth 4) mark him as an Old Testament saint.

In those days people conducted all serious negotiations at Bethlehem's town gate, which functioned rather like the town hall today. It was a common social meeting place, and since witnesses were readily available there, it was also a place where men made normal business transactions. There Boaz waits, knowing that sooner or later the other kinsman-redeemer is sure to show up. The other man's name is not known to us, but we do know that he is only interested in the privileges of the position, not in the sacrifices it might call for.

The Ceremony Continues

Once the other kinsman-redeemer appears, Boaz invites him to sit down. Then come important details in the ceremony of bygone times. Ceremony is important. It is an essential part of every nation and every form of culture. It is highly important for missionaries to recognize this fact and to take a tribe's anthropology (for example) into account. Otherwise they will find it hard to distinguish that which is purely cultural from that which is evil. Purchase of land, marriage customs and many other aspects of human life will be governed either by law or by custom, by an intricate system of rules, written or unwritten, governing the regulation of life.

Boaz assembles ten of the town elders because, in early Israelite culture, what is about to take place requires witnesses of unimpeachable honesty (4:2). With the ten elders a full court is present to observe the legality of the proceedings, and Boaz turns and addresses his fellow kinsman-redeemer. During the whole ceremony Boaz is very careful to be strictly honest. If he fails to reveal the advantages of the deal, he could be accused of being misleading, but he must also present the responsibilities that would follow, dealing carefully with the pros and the cons. He opts to present the positive side first—the acquisition of property.

> Then he said to the kinsman-redeemer, "Naomi, who has come back from Moab, is selling the piece of land that belonged to our brother Elimelech. I thought I should bring the matter to your attention and suggest that you buy it in the presence of these seated here and in the presence of the elders of my people. If you will redeem it, do so. But if you will not, tell me, so I will know. For no one has the right to do it except you, and I am next in line."
>
> "I will redeem it," he said. (4:3-4)

So far, so good. But Boaz's fellow kinsman-redeemer knows only the advantages of his choice, not the disadvantages. It is important that Boaz, if he is to be absolutely honest and display the qualities of the kinsman-redeemer to come, give him the full story. So he spells out what else the deal will involve. The first-in-line will also have to redeem Ruth, to marry her and, because she is of childbearing years, carry on through her the line of Elimelech and Mahlon. Elimelech's family name would in this way not disappear into obscurity. The kinsman-redeemer would, in effect, be carrying on a dead man's ancestry through Ruth. Boaz clearly explains that this would be a major responsibility.

At this, the kinsman-redeemer says, "Then I cannot redeem it because I might endanger my own estate. You redeem it yourself. I cannot do it" (4:6). The kinsman-redeemer refuses because his own estate might pass into obscurity, eclipsed by that of his dead relative.

But Boaz can and will redeem the property and Ruth, in spite of the fact that he may be running an equally big risk. *Never did he expect that his name would be recorded and remembered for centuries!*

Boaz is presented to us in the book of Ruth as exemplifying the virtues of our greater Redeemer. Redemption, mentioned many times in differing ways throughout the book, is the key to understanding the story. The two people who most reflect redemptive love are Boaz, an Israelite, and Ruth, a citizen of Moab. Ruth abandons her people, forsakes her gods, wants to die where Naomi will die and to worship Naomi's God. Acting as they do, they anticipate the saving work of Christ, of whom they are as much ancestors as was Abraham himself.

When God called Abraham to sacrifice Isaac God said, "Through your offspring all nations on earth will be blessed, because you have obeyed me" (Genesis 22:18). *Because you have obeyed me.* The words are highly significant. Obedience implies trust in God's person, and trustful obedience has always been a key to salvation. Salvation from sin, though it came through the Jews, was never intended for them alone. It was to be for "all nations" (Genesis 26:4).

Salvation and the Jews

Salvation by redemption has never been for Jews only. Every tribe, people and nation on earth has incorporated into its traditions some aspect of what Christians call the gospel. Some tribal peoples know only that there is a Creator God and that he is altogether good. He is the God of every people and tribe on earth. Every tribe with which I was in contact as a tribal missionary knew at least that much.

Polynesian peoples know from a constellation they see in the sky that a *redeemer* God exists. The discovery of natural methods of communication in a tribe can have dramatic results. Some years ago I met Monty, a Maori who was an official in the New Zealand educational service. Among the Maoris, one cultural method of communication is the war dance. A true Maori war dance choreographed by Monty was based on Ephesians 6:10-18.

In the first of two villages where it was performed, the vast majority of the people accepted Christ within a week, and in another village everyone did. Clearly the gospel was most effective when communicated through a war dance among Maori people, because of the significance of war dances in that society. Tribal peoples, relatively unaffected by our "scientific outlook," already know a great deal about principalities and powers in the heavenly places. Throughout the history of the human race God has planned the salvation of all peoples and nations. In each people or language group there is usually a key to communicating the gospel. With the Maori it was a war dance. So the Father of us all was running forward to the tribe to gather them in his arms.

Bruce Olson—Bruchko, as tribal people dubbed him—suffered greatly in finding out what communication method was used among the Motilone Indian tribe in Colombia. Eventually, victory came on a night when death by evil spirits seemed inevitable. But the one Christian convert, Bobby, had discovered that as he sang the "Jesus song" he would be protected.

Jesus is in my mouth;
I have a new speech.
Jesus is in my mouth;
No one can take him from me.

I speak Jesus' words.
I walk in Jesus' steps.
I am Jesus' boy;
He has filled my stomach,
and I am no longer hungry.[1]

In the tribal understanding, death removes all speech. So to say that "Jesus is in my mouth" is to confidently proclaim life in the midst of danger. Bobby sang and was protected, but for the first time in the tribe's history the rest of them also were protected from the malice of evil spirits. Several months later others asked to sing the song too. After fourteen hours of singing, the tribal chief commented, looking at the singer, Bobby, "You've communicated a true new item. I, too, want to suspend myself in Jesus. I want to pull his blood over my deception."[2] In that tribe, songs were sung as a means of communicating information. Again, the Father of us all was delighted to gather them all into his arms.

Don Richardson's books *Eternity in Their Hearts* and *Lords of the Earth* are rich with the same theme. Likewise early Chinese emperors, about 2000 B.C., practiced the worship of Shang'Ti, the Heavenly Ruler, making annual sacrifices to him. Ethel Nelson and Richard Broadberry's *Genesis and the Mystery Confucius Couldn't Solve* gives many evidences of an early knowledge of God.

The Birth of a Son in Bethlehem

For some reason I find the last few verses of Ruth 4 particularly moving. I am not altogether sure why, but they incline me to tears of joy. Is it senility? Or the wonder of God's faithfulness? Once Boaz claims his right as kinsman-redeemer, the witnesses confirm the arrangement with a stirring blessing.

> Then the elders and all those at the gate said, "We are witnesses. May the LORD make the woman who is coming into your home like Rachel and Leah, who together built up the house of Israel. May you have standing in Ephrathah, and be famous in Bethlehem. Through the offspring the LORD gives you by this young woman, may your family be like that of Perez, whom Tamar bore to Judah." (4:11-12)

Then Boaz and Ruth are married. Soon thereafter Boaz "went to her," as any new husband does. The following phrase appeals to our sense of a happy ending: "And the LORD *enabled her* to conceive, and she gave birth to a son" (4:13). A son is male, and maleness was the way by which the line was continued in Hebrew reckoning. Thus Mahlon's line would be continued because of Boaz's kindness and God's blessing.

The Lord *enabled her* to conceive? Of course. God begins life, and God ends life. He is the First and the Last in this sense also, the beginner and the ender of all human existence. Life begins at his command and ends at his command. I have known many occasions when women have sought prayer to conceive a child. The classic biblical example of course is Hannah (1 Samuel 1). Some women seek medical investigation only to be told by the gynecologist, "There is no reason for you not to conceive." On occasion I have known of women who have been told that they will not be able to conceive because of gynecological problems. Yet even in those cases people prayed and conception took place.

God is all in all in such matters, and he is a prayer-hearing

God. Hannah prayed. In 2 Kings 4 we read of the barren Shunammite woman who was astonished by Elisha's announcement that she would conceive and bear a son within a year's time. To her joy she did, and her son grew. But she was devastated when he suddenly died. Again, Elisha intervened in prayer. The woman found that Elisha's God, who could produce conception, was also the Lord over death. Elisha restored the boy to life. The New Testament shows that Jesus finally triumphed over death, and we are to do greater works even than he.

I have never raised the dead, but I have known of several people who have had such experiences. Certainly Smith-Wigglesworth, who had no denominational affiliation, did.[3] Our God is the Lord of life and death. In the end he proved to be the Lord of life to Naomi.

> The women said to Naomi: "Praise be to the LORD, who this day has not left you without a kinsman-redeemer. May he become famous throughout Israel! He will renew your life and sustain you in your old age. For your daughter-in-law, who loves you and who is better to you than seven sons, has given him birth." (4:14-15)

You will notice that the women in this case are addressing Naomi, but they focus not on her but on the one who has been the agent in rescuing her, the kinsman-redeemer. Of the baby boy they say, "May he become famous throughout Israel!" as he certainly did through his son and grandson.

But the women also speak of Ruth. They tell Naomi, "She loves you and is better than seven sons." Naomi's happiness by now is growing rapidly. The bitterness of her dark past had only been a part of her salvation. Now light floods into Naomi's dark world, and a deep sense of fulfillment is replacing the hopelessness of the time in Moab. She senses that God's judgment of her is now a thing of the past. In cultural terms, she has been released. God the Father specializes in finding people.

> Then Naomi took the child, laid him in her lap and cared for him. The women living there said, "Naomi has a son." And they named him Obed. He was the father of Jesse, the father of David. (4:16-17)

David, of course, became king over Israel. And centuries later, from the line of David, was born the one who would be the kinsman-redeemer for us all—Jesus.

Christ's Ancestry

Three women existed as remarkable antecedents of Christ. Naomi herself had been very bitter. Would not a more perfect ancestor be better? No. We are all imperfect. As a Moabite, Ruth hardly qualified as an ancestor. But when you think of it, the prostitute Rahab may be the most remarkable of all (see Joshua 2 and 6:25). "What!" you exclaim. "A prostitute is an ancestor of Christ?" Yes, and why not? That is what redemption is all about.

We have a wrong notion of the sacred, what I call a stained-glass-church-window notion. Stained-glass windows can give us the impression that the figures they bear are not like we are, sinners. Having transcended our sinful state, stained-glass saints are superior. Jesus came for sinners, and sinners were those among whom he was born. In his baptism he chose to be *identified with sinners.* Saints are merely redeemed and rescued sinners. Though he was sinless himself, his human ancestry includes all sorts of sinners and saints. He was constantly surrounded by sinners, for God was not rejecting human beings but saving them.

Rahab was not a stained-glass saint, just a former prostitute and a faithful believer, whom God blessed by making her an ancestor of Jesus. Matthew 1:5-6 tells us: "Salmon [was] the father of Boaz, *whose mother was Rahab,* Boaz [was] the father of Obed, whose mother was Ruth, Obed [was] the father of Jesse, and Jesse [was] the father of King David." Thus we see that Ruth, a person who would have been despised by the Jews of her day since she was a Gentile, and Rahab, who would be looked down on by many Christians today, were chosen by God to be in the line that bore both David and Christ.

Christ's purpose in dying was to conquer death and to snatch from Satan's cruel hand the power of death. He did so by rising bodily from the dead and ascending to the Father's side. The way is now open for us to follow. A way of salvation lies open to all humankind, including prostitutes and bitter women! No sinner—male or female—is too vile for God to redeem. At the heart of the Scripture is the song of the redeemed.

In ancient Jewish society the male line is the more important one in genealogy, but do we assume then that God is not concerned about the women who bear men's children? There is substance to the saying "The hand that rocks the cradle rules the world." Christ will rule one day, and soon. I do not for one moment suppose that his human mother, Mary, would presume to tell him how to rule, but I know that a sovereign God chooses with great care the women who bear certain men. He is a sovereign God.

Naomi did not know it, but God had an overruling purpose for Elimelech's family to spend time in Moab. How else would certain ancestors both of David and of Christ have been in the line? God is concerned about *his Son!* He is not merely being kind and gracious to certain women—though time and again he has proved that he is and will always be. Yet his prime concern has all along been with Jesus. Some of those ancestors may mystify us. But we shall know one day that there were no mistakes in his choices.

5

Salvation Revealed

The New is in the Old concealed: the Old is in the New revealed.

Do not think that I have come to abolish the Law or the Prophets;
I have not come to abolish them but to fulfill them.
I tell you the truth, until heaven and earth disappear,
not the smallest letter, not the least stroke of a pen,
will by any means disappear from the Law until
everything is accomplished. (Matthew 5:17-18)

God is a loving God—he *is* love. His love is a holy love, and I, for one (I am ashamed to say), am sometimes afraid of that love. I believe that Naomi probably was also. Ruth, I suppose, just accepted it, whereas Naomi recognized that she deserved his judgment. *And so she did!* For all along, she had never been in control. God had. She had been managing things that should not and *could* not be managed—she should have inquired of God. Instead she led her loved ones into temptation above what they could stand. But God still loved her. What he gave her was not judgment but discipline, the discipline reserved for those he loves.

In the Hotel Bathroom

Lorrie and I were staying in a hotel once. I had been very, very angry with her the previous night, and though my rage was inexcusable, I gave way to it. Because I was still angry, my anger robbed me of any hope of sleep. I'm sure the fact that I couldn't sleep was divinely controlled—that is the kind of God I believe in. By 1:15 a.m. I gave up. I went to the bathroom (not for the usual reasons), closed the door and switched on the light, trying not to disturb Lorrie. I sat on the toilet—it was the only place to sit—and asked God why I still felt so very angry.

He said, "I love you."

I didn't want to hear that. I didn't want his love, because I recognized I was not worthy of it. Instead I opened my Bible, to look for something that was not about God's love for me. I had previously been planning to expound Luke 15—the three parables about the love of God that feature the shepherd, the woman and the father. Obviously that would not do if I was too mad to receive God's love myself. I would be a hypocrite. Preaching is solemn business. So, like a Pharisee, I began to search the Scriptures for more suitable material.

The Spirit said, "I want you to dwell in my love."

I stopped searching and began to realize I was in a mess. I turned up the passage he quoted from John's Gospel: "As the Father has loved me, so have I loved you. Now remain in my love. If you obey my commands, you will remain in my love, just as I have obeyed my Father's commands and remain in his love. I have told you this so that my joy may be in you and that your joy may be complete" (John 15:9-11).

Right then I had no joy. I was very weary and still somewhat angry. I could have used some sleep but knew that sleep was out of the question. Suddenly I remembered a verse in the Song of Songs:

"Thy love is better than wine." *What on earth does that mean?* I had thought to myself many years before, until I remembered the sensation of drinking port wine at Christmas in England. We would relax in the "sitting room" and drink a glass of port, while my father and my uncle smoked cigars. The smell of cigars was wonderful. My father used them only at Christmas, and to me they expressed and gave me a sense of Christmas. There in the bathroom I remembered the warm fuzzy feeling as the wine went down. It had been wonderful.

It dawned on me that you cannot abide in love without "drinking" it—like wine. Right then I did not want it, but I knew God wanted to administer his love to me. Well, somehow on that dreadful early morning, I "swallowed" and managed to get his love down. I shake my head in wonder at my reluctance now, for now I am full of joy. His joy is in me, and my joy is complete— just as the passage in John's Gospel says. Even in my rebellion I wanted to obey his commands. Knowing he loved me was enough to bring about a change in my will. Obediently swallow- ing the love brought peace, then joy. I knew then that in spite of my reluctance, I had to preach on Luke 15. For the Shepherd had heaved me onto his shoulders, ignoring the stench of my sin, because he was so relieved to have me there.

Redemption Springs from God's Love

The love of Ruth and Boaz for each other included sex, but it was based on something far more solid and enduring than sex alone. It included kindness, gentleness, tenderness and mutual respect. God's love is the same, only infinitely better. In the book of Ruth we see Calvary anticipated, for in Calvary we see the love of God the Three-in-One. Love caused the Son to obey willingly the Father's loving redemptive mission to humanity.

The Holy Spirit revealed that same love to us. So all three members of the Trinity are involved. God is One, but within the Godhead is that which we cannot understand—three persons who are one in purpose, in thought and in determination.

Luke 15 beautifully portrays that focused love in the parables of the father, the shepherd and the woman. Many people equate the shepherd in the parable with Jesus, the woman in the parable of the lost coin with the Holy Spirit, and the waiting father with God the Father.

That Jesus told these three stories together indicates his emphasis on their common message. Hebrew scholars tell me that in Hebrew one can emphasize something by repeating an adjective. Thus in Revelation 4:8 (Greek not Hebrew—but in John's thought still Hebrew) the thrice-repeated word *holy* would give the emphasis of very, very, *very:* "Each of the four living creatures had six wings and was covered with eyes all around, even under his wings. Day and night they never stop saying: 'Holy, holy, holy is the Lord God Almighty, who was, and is, and is to come.' " A thrice-repeated parable would also be very, *very* important. Curiously, both holiness and love are not exactly God's attributes. They constitute his essential being. He *is* holiness, and he *is* love.

The Source of the Three Parables

The context of the parables is found in the first two verses of Luke 15.

> Now the tax collectors and "sinners" were all gathering around to hear him. But the Pharisees and the teachers of the law muttered, "This man welcomes sinners and eats with them." (Luke 15:1-2)

The parables are Christ's response to the attitude of the scholars and the Pharisees—and we the church have much in common with Pharisees. Some of their contemporaries would regard tax collectors as traitors to Israel. The sinners were probably varied. They might include prostitutes, drunks and others; today this group would also include drug addicts. All these people on the seamy side of life found themselves attracted to this man Jesus.

On the whole, churches do not attract sinners. In this respect churches differ from Jesus. Did Jesus seek to attract the "sinners"? Was he sinner-friendly? Or could it be that there was a deeper quality in Jesus, an integrity, an honesty and a love that drew sinners to him? After all, Jesus never said things just to please the crowd! He was not that sort—just the opposite, in fact. He was not afraid to castigate sin, in any form or person. His no-holds-barred teaching hit out not just at disreputable sinners despised by society but also at scribes and Pharisees. He cursed the sinful Pharisees with a series of woes (Matthew 23). But to most sinners he showed courtesy and love.

In North America, society has always tended to classify people. We see the poor as not being above the suspicion of shiftlessness or even of manipulation of the system, whereas some of the poor are genuinely victims of their circumstances and many work hard. Jesus plainly sees the poor as those who should be the first to receive the "good news" of the gospel (Matthew 11:5; Luke 4:18; 7:22). That certainly challenges us to look with new eyes.

We all like to feel that we are respectable. In any society we tend to divide sins into two sorts—the "respectable" sins of the upstanding and the "disreputable" sins of the lawless and poor. Some Christian people see matters in terms of who is respectable and who is not, rather than who are sinners and who are not. On the whole, respectable sinners are the worse sinners in God's sight. Jesus told the following parable to make this very point.

Two men went up to the temple to pray, one a Pharisee and the other a tax collector. The Pharisee stood up and prayed about himself: "God, I thank you that I am not like other men—robbers, evildoers, adulterers—or even like this tax collector. I fast twice a week and give a tenth of all I get." But the tax collector stood at a distance. He would not even look up to heaven, but beat his breast and said, "God, have mercy on me, a sinner."

I tell you that this man, rather than the other, went home justified before God. For everyone who exalts himself will be humbled, and he who humbles himself will be exalted (Luke 18:10-14).

Respectability exalts the respectable. Jesus was speaking in the presence of the Pharisees and scholars on this occasion. They were criticizing him for his association with disreputable people. He wanted to make it clear, both to Pharisees (doctors of the law) and to sinners generally, that salvation is due to God's loving kindness, and that this loving kindness, this grace and mercy, has to be swallowed in some sense. But our pride, our self-sufficiency and our feelings of superiority—that we are *better* than other people—makes it difficult for us to swallow.

"Respectability" can afflict anyone. Sadly, even many (but by no means all) of our own Bible scholars and theologians are no different from the Pharisees and scholars of their day. They share the same respectability and unwillingness to receive God's love. They know the theory but choke and splutter in trying to swallow divine love. I have choked on it myself but am making progress at last.

Such people are the weeds Jesus spoke about (Matthew 13:14-30; 13:36-43). They seem unable even to see the need to do what

Paul recommends: "Examine yourselves to see whether you are in the faith; test yourselves. Do you not realize that Christ Jesus is in you—unless, of course, you fail the test?" (2 Corinthians 13:5).

When the Matthew passages about wheat and tares strike home to you, it comes as a shock. We commonly assume we are among the redeemed, but we fail to attempt the self-examination Paul recommends. The parables were to explain God's motive in providing redemption.

The First Parable

How did Jesus respond to the Pharisees and teachers of the law? He first told them this story:

> Suppose one of you has a hundred sheep and loses one of them. Does he not leave the ninety-nine in the open country and go after the lost sheep until he finds it? And when he finds it, he joyfully puts it on his shoulders and goes home. Then he calls his friends and neighbors together and says, "Rejoice with me; I have found my lost sheep." (Luke 15:4-6)

We all are inclined to see Jesus in the good shepherd. But let us look more closely at the parable. The shepherd had lost one sheep in a hundred. The word *lost* can be understood in two senses. Sometimes I recognize when walking that I am not where I thought I was. I gaze around and know that I must have missed a path in the forest or gone down the wrong street in town. Everything around is strange, unfamiliar. I am *lost*—that is, I have "lost my way."

The other sense in which we use the word has to do with the person who loses something. It is in this sense that the word *lost* is used in all three parables. The shepherd lost a sheep, the woman lost a coin, the father lost a son. What is interesting about this is that when we lose something or someone, the loss assumes a disproportionate amount of our attention.

I lose my car keys from time to time. Similarly, my wife is inclined to lose whichever purse she happens to be using at the moment. When I lose my car keys I vary between irritation and rage. I want everybody to be as concerned as I am myself. I say, "I am absolutely sure they were in my right-hand trouser pocket. *I know they were.* And they're gone! They've just disappeared. I've searched everywhere, and I know they're lost."

My wife is inclined to behave similarly over her purse. Of course, eventually my keys turn up. Just as the concern was disproportionate, so is the relief. I experience a sense of joy accompanied with the feeling of having been very silly.

Yet this is exactly how God feels about lost sinners—not silly, but relieved. It is of no consequence to him that you are one of several billion people. He cares in an individual way for each of us. We should feel the same way about each of our own children—all different, yet all equally loved. Indeed the fact that they all differ, that all are unique, makes sense to us, as it does to God, who cares with equally passionate concern for each of us. The fact that the parables go from one of a hundred lost, then one of ten, to finally one of two teaches us that very lesson. God apparently does not think of us as a mass, or if he does, he is more concerned about each of us as individuals. How he is capable of doing so baffles us. After all, *he is God,* and we will never figure him out.

> Lord, Thou hast here Thy ninety and nine,
> Are they not enough for Thee?
> But the shepherd made answer, "This of mine
> Has wandered away from me."

God is disproportionately concerned about the lost sheep. The shepherd is so concerned that he leaves the other sheep unattended in the open country. God's concern is like that. Remember, Middle Eastern shepherds knew their sheep by name and would lead them, whereas we Westerners drive them. So the shepherd abandons the ninety-nine in his overwhelming concern with the one missing sheep. He travels over the extremely rugged and treacherous wilderness, experiencing significant hardship, pain and danger which parallels (in kind though not in degree) Jesus' own suffering.

If the shepherd represents Jesus, as I believe he does, what do we say about the love behind Christ's own sacrifice? He was blindfolded and mocked in the garb of a king. Roman soldiers callously put him through a public hazing and lashing. Then, totally stripped and exposed, he endured the cruelest form of punishment ever invented—iron stakes were driven through his wrists and ankles.

All this he did for our sakes. He is not to be pitied, because he did all that as the Mighty Conqueror over the powers of hell and of death. But because he was also the Holy Lamb of God, death could not retain its hold on him, the lord of death was defeated, both on our behalf and on the behalf of all the Old Testament saints.

But none of the ransomed ever knew
How deep were the waters crossed;
Nor how dark was the night that the Lord passed through
Ere he found his sheep that was lost.
Eventually, however,
There arose a glad cry to the gates of Heaven,
"Rejoice! I have found my sheep!"
And the angels echoed around the throne,
"Rejoice! For the Lord brings back his own!"

None of the ransomed ever knew how deep the waters were. We probably never will know, for we will always lack the capacity to understand the sufferings of a holy God. But we may worship him with all the adoration of our hearts. Even our service will in that day be a form of worship.

Joy and the Rejoicing

God rejoices over us with great joy, and this is precisely what the shepherd in the story did. Such was his joy that his step lightened. I have seen Sunday-school literature in which the sheep becomes (quite understandably) a lamb, a dear, cuddly little thing with white nylon wool flecked with pink and blue. But the shepherd in the parable hefted a heavy, stinky sheep onto his shoulders. Stinky? Sheep do smell, you know. Moreover, they often have a caked mess around their rear end. You smell what's on your shoulders.

You say, "Well, you don't have to *mention* such matters." No? Sin is every bit as objectionable to God as our caked garbage would be to that shepherd. But the fact is that he doesn't care, so great is his joy in finding what was lost. Indeed, he still has energy to spare when he gets home. Joy has to be shared, and in this case he runs round to his friends and neighbors to invite them to celebrate with him. And that is what angels do as they glimpse the unfathomable— the joy of God. And so the parable concludes:

> I tell you that in the same way there is more rejoicing in heaven over one sinner who repents than over ninety-nine righteous persons who do not need to repent. (Luke 15:7)

The Second Parable

The second parable concerns a woman who sweeps the floor in search of a lost coin—one of ten.

Or suppose a woman has ten silver coins and loses one. Does she not light a lamp, sweep the house and search carefully until she finds it? And when she finds it, she calls her friends and neighbors together and says, "Rejoice with me; I have found my lost coin." (Luke 15:8-9)

Commentaries give various explanations about the purpose of the coins. Were they for her burial? Were they used in life as a head ornament, a sort of crown? Did they represent her life savings? But as we have already seen, the important point is that all her concern is over what she has lost. The nine are safe. One is missing. The sum would not be complete without that one. In her disproportionate concern over the one, the woman represents how God feels about lost sinners. He longs for their return.

Why, if Jesus explains that this represents God's attitude to sinners, does he use a woman? One reason to do so might be to illustrate the difference between roles and states of being. He does so because both masculine and feminine were within God before sexual beings existed. Sex and gender are not the same as male and female. Sex has to do with men and women and their physical differences. Gender has to do with the spirit world which preceded the creation of sex and all the self-multiplying creatures that surround us. *Spiritual beings came first.* He who is Spirit created all things. Gender is primordial.

Spiritual beings have gender but lack sexual characteristics—except on those rare occasions when spirit beings take on human form. Jesus, for instance, was a male and had the physical characteristics of a male. He had to be either a man or a woman. His being male did and does not mean females are inferior but that their roles differ. In Christ there is neither male nor female, and in the resurrection even our bodies will not have a procreative function (see Matthew 22:30 and Luke 20:35). No sex in heaven? Jesus says not.

Feminists fail to understand that submission does not necessarily imply inferiority. The masculine *initiates*. The Father initiates and the Son responds, doing what he sees the Father do. As Jesus said, "I tell you the truth, the Son can do nothing by himself; he can do only what he sees his Father doing, because whatever the Father does the Son also does" (John 5:19). Thus God the Father initiates, and God the Son responds. Jesus submits and obeys the will of the Father. The Son does not become inferior to the Father by responding to him, or by submitting to him, or by accepting a feminine role in relation to the Father. When Christ, as supreme conqueror of the powers of hell, accomplishes the task the Father gave him, "the end will come, *when he hands over the kingdom to God the Father* after he has destroyed all dominion, authority and power" (1 Corinthians 15:24).

The role of the Spirit in relation to the roles of the Father and Son is feminine (not *female,* but feminine), just as the Son submits to the Father. But in relation to us, because he initiates, the Spirit is masculine. We take the feminine role and submit to him.

Representing God the Holy Spirit, the woman with the lost coin lights a lamp. Why? She lights it to see better. The house likely has no windows, and the corners are dark. She sweeps, under furniture, in corners, searching for what she lost. She is determined to seek until she finds it. And again, just as the concern may seem disproportionate, so the joy when she finds her coin is disproportionate. In her happiness at finding the thing she had lost (the sinner who had strayed from her protective care), she runs to her friends and neighbors to share her good news.

And again, Jesus repeats the words, "In the same way, I tell you, there is rejoicing in the presence of the angels of God over one sinner who repents" (15:10).

God throws a party in our honor. We may not feel worthy of such a celebration, but that is God's spontaneous reaction nonetheless. When we respond to his initiative, he turns the music up high, brings in vast quantities of food and drink and invites all his friends to rejoice with him. We mean that much to him.

6

Weeping
for Joy

Cruelty has a human heart, and Jealousy a human face;
Terror the human form divine, and Secrecy the human dress.[1]

The story of the prodigal's return is the story of God's love for human beings. The nature of God's holy love and its importance in our lives cannot be exaggerated. It is the motive behind the crucifixion. It is very, *very* important. Unless we not only understand but *experience* that love, I question our effectiveness in trying to communicate it. It is the center of all gospel preaching.

Jesus gives us all three parables to teach us what the love of God is like—the same reason he gave us the book of Ruth. The distinctness of Father, Son and Spirit and their great love for humans shines through in the three parables.

As I mentioned earlier, in English when we wish to express extreme good we can say, "That was *very, very* good," whereas in some Middle Eastern languages one may repeat an adjective several times to give the same effect. In Isaiah 6:3 we read of Isaiah's first vision and of the cry "Holy, holy, holy is the LORD Almighty; the whole earth is full of his glory." We also sometimes speak of a "thrice holy God." All of this is for emphasis. Likewise, the three parables about God's love suggest that their common message is of very great importance.

Wishing the Old Man Dead

Jesus emphasizes his point a third time in the parable of the prodigal son.

> There was a man who had two sons. The younger one said to his father, "Father, give me my share of the estate." So he divided his property between them. (Luke 15:11-12)

Henri Nouwen wrote a book titled *The Return of the Prodigal Son*. It is a sensitive examination of the implications of this story seen through Nouwen's meditations as he gazes at one of Rembrandt's paintings—his second and last on the same theme of the prodigal's return. Nouwen quotes Kenneth Bailey, who had traveled "from Morocco to India and from Turkey to the Sudan," countries whose peasant cultures share much in common with each other and even with the peasant culture of the ancient Middle East. In each country Bailey asked the same question: What would be the implications of a son asking his father for his portion of the family inheritance? In every country in which he traveled, Bailey got the same reaction.

"Has anyone ever made such a request in your village?"
"Never!"
"Could anyone make such a request?"
"Impossible!"
"If anyone ever did, what would happen?"
"His father would beat him, of course!"

"Why?"

"The request means—he wants his father to die."[2]

Bailey explains that in making the request, the son is also asking for the right to dispose of the inheritance immediately. Normally the father would retain that right—the right to make use of his own money—until his death. Thus to make the request is the equivalent of saying, "I wish you were dead."

The God of heaven loves us all, yet we all treat his resources as if they were our own by right. Many already have wished God dead, while others believe he either is dead or else has never existed. The marvel of the parable lies here.

The Distant Country

If we doubted that the prodigal wished his father were dead, he makes his attitude abundantly clear when he chooses to get as far away from his father as he can.

> Not long after that, the younger son got together all he had, set off for a distant country and there squandered his wealth in wild living. (Luke 15:13)

It seems that everything about his father irritates him. He is going to get away from the old man for good and forever. Plainly, he wants nothing more to do with him. Or so, in his youth, he thinks.

Distant countries have an allure. I know; I have lived in several. For a while I was intrigued by the amazing cultural differences that distinguish one culture from another, even when they share a common language. Yet after some time I began to discover that human nature is the same the world over. Canada is quite different from the United States, which is in turn quite different from Mexico. Black culture differs from white. But when you get down to basics, people the world over actually differ very little. I've taken years to search what is in my own heart, and within me I have discovered murder and every other evil passion. In the deepest sense, we are all the same. We share the same sinful nature and are all capable of the same sins.

When, I wonder, did the prodigal first decide on a distant land? Before his request, or after he had made it? I rather think he had determined to go abroad beforehand. My suspicion is that he would have left whether or not his father agreed to the bargain. Knowing he would get the money only made the matter easier. In any case, distant countries hold romantic allure. Remoteness and cultural distinctiveness promise excitement. Moab had an allure for Elimelech and Naomi. In a sense they were prodigals. God did not—and would not—stop them from exercising their freedom, even though in so doing they went against his will.

When the son realizes he will be okay financially, his eyes brighten and his spirits rise. Exciting prospects please us. Surely his anticipation builds while he plans his journey, purchases what he needs, then finally sets off.

Love, Longing and Delight

The point of the parables, as I have said repeatedly, is our lost focus on divine love. Yes, it is love combined with judgment/discipline. But it is passionate love of inestimable desire and longing. A parent's longing for a missing child can give us only an inadequate idea of God's love for the human beings he has lost—and for those he will lose eternally.

And yes, this love is mixed with anger. In a park in Paris, France, I once pleaded for a second son. I prayed, "God, give me another son—provided he will live to your glory."

The Lord replied, "To my glory *or to yours?*" He then asked me, "What about me with Adam?"

With dismay I saw that God knew beforehand not only the

tragedy of a lost Eden but all the horrors down the many millennia that have followed.

I asked him, "What do you mean?"

Immediately he gave me a mental picture of prison walls and a prison gate, and I knew what he was showing me.

"D'you mean he'll go to jail?"

But there was no answer.

Finally, as my knees grew soaked from the damp earth and I grew anxious, I said, "Okay, I'll have him."

Two months later my wife conceived. For a while I forgot about the conversation in the joy of having a second child. But it became clear after four or five years that yes, this *was* the child God had offered me. As three more children followed, all reasonably obedient, this one stood out. Years later, the telephone rang, and when it was this son, I always knew. There were times, I confess, when I would walk away from the telephone. Sometimes I would be angry, but at other times I despaired, or I had no idea of what to say. For his constant question would be "When will I become like you guys? What can I do?"

He drank. He did drugs. He lived on the street and was often in fights—and yes, he did time in jail. Once when he was very drunk he came to see me. He said, "Dad, you know I'm drunk, don't you?"

I nodded.

"Well, I've come to say something that I can't say when I'm sober. *Dad, I love you!*"

I loved him too. We get angriest with the people we most love.

A Fool, His Money and Taxes

In the King James version of Scripture we read that the prodigal "wasted his substance with riotous living" (Luke 15:13). The money is wasted rather than *used,* for "a fool and his money are soon parted." This young man soon squanders his wealth. But that raises the question of how money should be used. Exactly what constitutes the proper use of our money? To whom does all money belong?

Trying to "catch Jesus in something he said," spies from the Pharisees and doctors of the law once asked Jesus a similar question.

"Is it right for us to pay taxes to Caesar or not?"

He saw through their duplicity and said to them, "Show me a denarius. Whose portrait and inscription are on it?"

"Caesar's," they replied.

He said to them, "Then give to Caesar what is Caesar's, and to God what is God's."

They were unable to trap him in what he had said there in public. And astonished by his answer, they became silent. (Luke 20:24-26)

The question they asked Christ remains with us because we still pay taxes. It is lawful, according to Jesus, to pay our taxes, even though governments can be infuriating in their use of our money. Even so, all money actually belongs to God, for it is God who controls the destinies of nations. Our greatest temptation is to use money in the service of Mammon. Mammon likes us to accumulate and hoard it. If this does not appeal, the powers of darkness encourage us to squander it on anything vicious.

The whole universe is God's. He has placed us in this world and would like us to serve him. Yet he never forces any of us to please him. We are free to go the way of the prodigal son, and we find out by bitter experience what will happen when we waste our substance in riotous living. We spend money uneasily when we lust for more, or we squander it on our pleasures and accumulate debt. God lets us learn by experience that giving money is better than receiving it. We must recognize that so far as our money goes, we will employ it either in the service of Mammon or in the service of God. It is impossible to sit on the fence where money is concerned. Jesus is absolutely clear about the matter: "No servant can serve two masters. Either he will hate the one and love the other, or he will be devoted to the one and despise the other. You cannot serve both God and Money" (Luke 16:13).

To some Christians, God gives the gift of multiplying wealth. Some of those same Christians fall under Mammon's allure and multiply wealth to benefit themselves. Unfortunately, the satisfaction of multiplied wealth quickly palls. So we do the only thing our hearts want, and we try to get more; a process of endless dissatisfaction begins. Others give generously to evangelistic efforts, feeling some satisfaction in giving, but still do not understand the ultimate freedom from Mammon. Still others take seriously the fact that all wealth is God's and inquire of him how he wants the wealth used.

If we do what God tells us, he will probably go on giving us more to spend. Hudson Taylor had a saying: "God's work done in God's way will never lack God's supply." To inquire of God how money should be used involves risks and may be very scary. But in the long run it will make us a source of great wealth for those around us. The flow through us will increase endlessly. Sadly, the prodigal son squanders his wealth on his vices and on those of his friends.

Life Teaches the Prodigal
The young man in the parable probably did not lack friends, for when you squander money, thinking it will last forever, fair-weather friends flock to you. But they are as quick to drift away once the fun ceases.

After he had spent everything, there was a severe famine in that whole country, and he began to be in need. So he went and hired himself out to a citizen of that country, who sent him to his fields to feed pigs. He longed to fill his stomach with the pods that the pigs were eating, but no one gave him anything. (Luke 15:14-16)

It is curious that when his money runs out, times of great economic hardship begin. Jesus, in telling the story, knows how these things work. His story is accurate, both about young men who throw money away and about how the world system operates.

The prodigal looks for employment and finds it. He does not do too well, however, for the employment consists of feeding pigs, a thing no self-respecting Jew would think of doing—unless he were stuck. Times are hard. He evidently does not earn enough to feed himself well and becomes hungry. I would imagine he loses weight. In the end he craves even the pigs' food. Does he get paid? Jesus does not tell us, but as we all know, in hard times employers of small enterprises—and even in large companies—may get stingy, cut our wages and postpone paying them.

Hunger is cruel. If you choose to fast, then the problem of hunger disappears fairly soon. But if you are fasting not by choice but because of circumstances, hunger's relentless grip on your body can be devastating. This was why what would normally have been disgusting to the young man now would look good to him. Pig food would become exceedingly appetizing in his circumstances.

Facing Hard Facts
In the end, the young man realizes he has been a fool. It commonly takes awhile for us to figure this out, because it is

never easy to admit even to ourselves that we have been wrong. He realizes that his father had been quite amazing in his attitude about the "share of the estate." Perhaps he sells some of his expensive clothing, hoping it will bring enough money for food, only to be terribly disappointed at the falling demand for clothing. Food matters more than clothes. Perhaps he begins to realize he is in a desperate situation. Problems of this sort begin slowly, as a rule.

> When he came to his senses, he said, "How many of my father's hired men have food to spare, and here I am starving to death! I will set out and go back to my father and say to him: Father, I have sinned against heaven and against you. I am no longer worthy to be called your son; make me like one of your hired men." So he got up and went to his father. (Luke 15:17-20)

He sees that he has pursued a wrong course and been at fault. His conscience troubles him. He makes up a speech, anticipating a return to home. He feels it would be wrong of him to expect to be treated as a son (how little he understands his father; indeed, how little so many of us understand our Father!), since he has sinned not only against his father but against God. So instead of being treated as a son, he decides he will ask for employment, making it quite clear that he knows he has no claim to sonship. He does not realize that he will always be a son, that nothing but death can change that fact. He cannot know that he will never have the chance to complete his speech, managing only to utter the first part of it.[3]

Love Also Watches and Waits

There is a mystery I cannot fully understand. Love searches. Clearly the first two parables teach it. But love also waits and watches. Both aspects of divine love are part of the whole. However much the Father longs, he has infinite patience. That is very hard to understand, for personally I am all of a dither between the two extremes—either all activity in my attempts to make something happen or all passivity in waiting for it. It becomes especially true where God has promised me something. The parables teach that God is both patient and active at the same time. He knows how to wait, but he also acts with precipitate suddenness.

> But while he was still a long way off, his father saw him and was filled with compassion for him; he ran to his son, threw his arms around him and kissed him. (Luke 15:20)

The father sees the son "while he was still a long way off." Why? Presumably because the father is watching from the rooftop. He has probably developed a habit, looking with inexpressible longing for his son's return. So he spends many hours watching and waiting. Is it really true that the love of God the Father is like that? The young man's father surely has had many disappointments, times when he sees a cloud of dust on a distant hilltop and begins to distinguish one or more figures, only to be disappointed.

But not this time. And he cannot hurry enough. Jewish men of worth in Christ's day never ran. They walked. Gravely, with great dignity. But the father in the parable *runs*. Such is his compassion that he casts dignity aside and moves with indecorous haste in his passion to welcome his son home. Then we read,

> The son said to him, "Father, I have sinned against heaven and against you. I am no longer worthy to be called your son."

> But the father said to his servants, "Quick! Bring the best robe and put it on him. Put a ring on his finger and sandals on his feet. Bring the fattened calf and kill it. Let's have a feast

and celebrate. For this son of mine was dead and is alive again; he was lost and is found." So they began to celebrate. (Luke 15:21-24)

Whether the father is shouting the orders as he runs or begins to shout orders afterward is unclear. In my mind I picture servants trailing their master as he yells to them. The best robe? Has it been long kept for such an occasion? A ring? A mark of authority and of sonship? Sandals? Is he walking barefoot? Is the footwear to distinguish him from the barefooted slaves and also mark him as a son?

The Celebration and the Pharisee

Once again there is a celebration, an extra-special celebration marked by the killing of a fattened calf. It is an indication of the heavenly Father's joy, a joy that is repeated over each sinner— over a bespectacled and timid clerk in Moscow or a seductive Mexican prostitute from the streets of Los Angeles.

I once wrote a book about repentance[4] and made the point that while the basis of our forgiveness is the confession of our sins (1 John 1:9), repentance comes when we truly realize how great the love of God toward us is. At that point strong men will dissolve in tears and sob. To sob is not the prerogative of women. When men begin to understand how great the love of God toward them is, they will howl like dogs. Whenever the awareness of God's great love overtakes me these days, I begin to cry. I have cried and sobbed more frequently in the last ten years of my life than ever before—for that one reason, because in a small way I am beginning to understand God's love.

We have to cry when we realize who is celebrating, and that he is celebrating because he is so delighted at the return of *one* son or daughter. We are beginning to find true fulfillment in the love of God toward us. To think of God's delight, of God's extreme joy—and over one sinner—blows one's delighted mind to shreds and tatters. It seems inconceivable. Yet apparently it is true.

But the story is not over.

Meanwhile, the older son was in the field. When he came near the house, he heard music and dancing. So he called one of the servants and asked him what was going on. "Your brother has come," he replied, "and your father has killed the fattened calf because he has him back safe and sound." The older brother became angry and refused to go in. (15:25-28)

In the second Rembrandt painting of the prodigal son, the older brother seems to be staring at the father. Like the father, the older son wears a rich red robe. His hands are folded and rest on his staff or walking stick. He also wears a richly ornamented turban. If he is indeed staring at the father (as he seems to be), his face expresses the cold incomprehension that the Pharisees had for Jesus. I struggle hard against Pharisaism myself. My sneering critical nature comes from an evil source, and I am determined to fight against it. Jesus urged us to adopt a servant attitude, the attitude from which all true authority arises.

The older brother typifies a Pharisee in his incomprehension of the father's heart of love. And, as mentioned above, the parables were occasioned by the critical presence of Pharisees and biblical scholars. Later in his life Jesus cursed the Pharisees sevenfold (Matthew 23)—for wanting to be seen as holy, for demanding the best seating, for loving public recognition from influential leaders.

Jesus compares their spirit (of which we all have a little) with whitewashed tombs (clean in appearance but rotting inside). He tells them that—unlike most churches today, which do not attract the sinners without trying to, as Jesus did, despite his uncompromising stand on sin—Pharisees go to any length to make a convert only to make him an even worse "son of hell" than they are themselves.

In addition to cursing Pharisees with seven curses or "woes," Jesus abuses them verbally in a way no self-respecting Christian would dream of doing today. Is that because he would verbally abuse us also? Are we all Pharisees? He berates them for their topsy-turvy logic, for their punctilious tithing and for their blindness. Like John the Baptist before him, Jesus hurls curses and insults at them:

> You snakes! You brood of vipers! How will you escape being condemned to hell? Therefore I am sending you prophets and wise men and teachers. Some of them you will kill and crucify; others you will flog in your synagogues and pursue from town to town. And so upon you will come all the righteous blood that has been shed on earth, from the blood of righteous Abel to the blood of Zechariah son of Berekiah, whom you murdered between the temple and the altar. (Matthew 23:33-35)

Jesus could be talking to us like this! When he speaks of his plans to send "prophets and wise men and teachers," in the same breath he predicts their persecution. We know from church history that the line of martyrs continued unabated and was even perpetuated by the church. Human nature does not change.

In the same way that it fell on the Jews, the blood of martyrs is now on the hands of the many churches that have made heretics out of righteous and godly people before killing them. For it seems that the most vicious persecutors are generally those who are displeased with the latest historical move of the Holy Spirit.

Thus certain Reformers persecuted the Mennonites, who practiced adult baptism and for this practice were deliberately drowned in the river. Magistrates and police carried out the sentence on behalf of Christians who practiced infant baptism. We have much blood on our hands in the church. At present in the West we confine ourselves to killing people's reputations, but this Pharisaic spirit has the same evil source: Satan.

In the Old Testament, Job's three friends, themselves self-righteous, assume that Job "must have" committed sin to cause the great tragedy that befell him. We are all inclined to similar criticisms. Yet all the while Job's righteousness was being proved by the suffering Satan inflicted on him (Job 1:9; 2:3, 9-10).

Mike Mason comments on the story, declaring that Job's comforters do what we all are inclined to do at times. Instead of comforting him, they

> were in their minds picking him to pieces, analyzing him up and down for faults, loopholes, and hidden sins, casting around in search of reasons for all the terrible things that had happened to him. And although we are told that these discreet gentlemen said nothing at all to Job for an entire week, is it not probable that they whispered confidentially among themselves?[5]

After all, their subsequent charges to him reflected the opinions they really held. Most of us have a hard time keeping our self-righteous opinions to ourselves, simply because self-righteousness is very hard to keep to oneself. Mason continues the discussion of Job's friends:

> Feeling overwhelmed, and scrambling to get a better fix on the problem, they will do the only safe thing: they will pull back and assume the stance of objective analysts. Naturally they will go about this in a very warm and godly way and with the best of intentions. . . . Yet without realizing it, by their clinical theorizing they are effectively withdrawing their human affections, at the very time when this intimate friendship is most needed.[6]

In addition to having the blood of the godly on our hands, we can be guilty of something equally evil when we engage in this sort of stuff. Human words, given originally that we might control the earth and its inhabitants, are far more powerful than we realize.

Weeping for Joy

I weep for joy these days. Especially when I read about the Incarnation. I actually weep over the fact that God became a human being. I cannot understand it. It amazes me. The fact that God would pass through the channel of a virgin's body *to become a human being* unmans me. Having had a prodigal son, I know what it's like when things improve. I know a lot more about God's love than I used to.

You see, when I was small, I was taught not only not to weep but *not even to cough!* That is how it was in those days in Britain. You were supposed to not bother adults by your weeping or coughing. So I learned not to. My parents were not bad people, just ordinary British Christians. I even learned not to feel! I guess God is releasing me from the errors of my early training. Now I know the release of weeping as well as of laughter.

All three parables end in celebration. All three end in joy, joy that now constantly erupts in the presence of the angels. So who rejoices? In the first parable the shepherd is reflecting Jesus, so I suppose we conclude that he rejoices. In the second, the woman rejoices on finding her lost coin; she reflects the Holy Spirit's joy.

In this third parable the father celebrates his son's return. And that son knows the joy of being loved undeservedly. What does the knowledge do for him? We can only surmise, for the parable stops short of telling us. The younger son did not even manage to get his speech out fully. Flooded with relief and happiness, his father interrupts with shouts to his servants. He is ecstatic, just as God the Father is at a sinner who turns to him.

But the older son shares none of the joy. Jesus describes this bitterness: "The older brother became angry and refused to go in." That is, he refuses to join in the celebration. His is a Pharisee's attitude.

> So his father went out and pleaded with him. But he answered his father, "Look! All these years I've been slaving for you and never disobeyed your orders. Yet you never gave me even a young goat so I could celebrate with my friends. But when this son of yours who has squandered your property with prostitutes comes home, you kill the fattened calf for him!"
>
> "My son," the father said, "you are always with me, and everything I have is yours. But we had to celebrate and be glad, because this brother of yours was dead and is alive again; he was lost and is found." (Luke 15:28-31)

Has he ever asked his father for a young goat with which to celebrate? It seems unlikely to me. People with a Pharisaic attitude are more inclined to take pride in how little they ask God for and how much they give to God. As we have just seen, they thank God that they are different.

The parable ends with the father's attempt to help his bitter, resentful son to understand how a father feels. But the words seem unconvincing. His protest seems lame. Why? Because many of us do not understand the father's heart and are ourselves unconvinced. Henri Nouwen felt that way. He says,

> It is hard for me to concede that this bitter, resentful, angry man might be closer to me in a spiritual way than the lustful younger brother. Yet the more I think about the elder son, the more I recognize myself in him. As the eldest son in my own family, I know well what it feels like to have to be a model son.[7]

The wonder of Christ's words lies in the fact that none of us need to go on playing the part of the resentful older brother. It may take time for the anger and bitterness to leave us. But we can begin by acknowledging these feelings as sin before God and telling him we need help in understanding his attitude. We need his gracious intervention in our lives. The nearest we will ever get to God is in and through Christ.

As we gaze on Christ, Scripture tells us that we will grow progressively more like him. "But we all, with open face beholding as in a glass the glory of the Lord, are changed into the same image from glory to glory, even as by the Spirit of the Lord" (2 Corinthians 3:18 KJV). I prefer the King James Version to the NIV in this instance, believing it to be more accurate. When the KJV tells us that we may behold Christ "as in a glass," it is talking about a mirror. Bronze mirrors were then used, and though they worked well, they gave nothing like the quality of reflection that our own mirrors give. We may indeed reflect Christ's glory by becoming increasingly like him, and the text actually uses a mirror image term.

Unless Christ appears to me in a vision, I see him only dimly, as I would perceive any spiritual reality. But I become more like him the more I contemplate[8] him, the more I think about him, the more I spend personal time with him and the more I let him love me. We become like the people with whom we spend a lot of time, and whom we love. I am changing by the grace of God. Though a long way from a perfect reflection, I am being changed "from one degree of glory to another."

In his goodness and mercy God wants to place his glory upon us all. All he requires of us is that we let him love us and that we spend time with him. All we have to do is to spend time in his presence, learning to gaze on him.

Notes

Chapter 1: Downhill to Bitterness
[1]Francis Thompson, *The Hound of Heaven* (New York: Dodd, Mead, 1922), p. 43.
[2]See Deuteronomy 25:5-6 to understand the legal principle. A good illustration of its outworking can be found in Genesis 38:6-26. Further discussion is also found in Matthew 22:23-32.

Chapter 2: Divine Providence
[1]Arthur E. Cundall and Leon Morris, *Judges and Ruth* (Downers Grove, Ill.: InterVarsity Press, 1968), p. 274.
[2]Ibid., p. 275.
[3]Ibid.

Chapter 3: Submission
[1]Boswell's *Life of Johnson,* July 9, 1763.
[2]Cundall and Morris, *Judges and Ruth,* p. 288.

Chapter 4: The Gospel and the Book of Ruth
[1]Bruce Olson, *Bruchko* (Orlando, Fla.: Creation House, 1993), p. 144.
[2]Ibid., pp. 140-46.
[3]Stanley Howard Frodsham, *Smith Wigglesworth, Apostle of Faith* (Springfield, Mo.: Gospel Publishing House, 1948), pp. 58-60.

Chapter 6: Weeping for Joy
[1]William Blake, "A Divine Image," in *Songs of Innocence.*
[2]Kenneth E. Bailey, *Poet and Peasant, and Through Peasant Eyes: A Literary-Cultural Approach to the Parables* (Grand Rapids, Mich.: Eerdmans, 1983), pp. 161-62, quoted in Henri Nouwen, *The Return of the Prodigal Son* (New York: Image/Doubleday, 1944), pp. 35-36.
[3]The succinct version of the parable makes it impossible to know what actually

happened. Perhaps Jesus intended this to be obscure, or perhaps he gave a full version of the younger son's speech when he first told the story. We don't know. In any case, the parable found in Luke's Gospel includes only a truncated version of the younger son's speech.

[4]John White, *Changing on the Inside* (Ann Arbor, Mich.: Servant, 1991).

[5]Mike Mason, *The Gospel According to Job* (Wheaton, Ill.: Crossway, 1994), p. 50.

[6]Ibid.

[7]Nouwen, *The Return of the Prodigal Son,* p. 69.

[8]In fact most editions of the NIV include the word *contemplate* in a footnote to 2 Corinthians 3:18 as an alternate translation of *reflect.*